MasterChef
GREEN

Adam O'Shepherd

with contributions from
MasterChef contestants

MasterChef
GREEN

90 veggie recipes to raise the ordinary to the extraordinary

with photography by
Adam and Marie O'Shepherd

BLOOMSBURY ABSOLUTE
LONDON · OXFORD · NEW YORK · NEW DELHI · SYDNEY

FOREWORD

'How did it all begin?'

That's the most frequent question I am asked about *MasterChef*.

Strangely enough, it started on the third floor of the production building at 20th Century Fox in Los Angeles. It was the early 1980s, and the famous actor and producer Mel Brooks was leading a pack of braying international creatives, mocking British food. 'There's no such thing as British cuisine; if you want a good meal in London you have to go Italian or French, or maybe Indian, but never British.'

I did my best to defend myself against the mockery, but in all honesty, this was the era of over-cooked meat, soggy vegetables and the ubiquitous greasy spoon cafés. Backed against the wall, but ever the fighter, I came up with my only defence: British cuisine is at its best in British homes. I started mentioning brandy butter at Christmas, fried leeks and bacon for Sunday breakfast, the custards, the cakes, stews and the amazing produce that we have in the UK. It may not have convinced them, but I convinced myself, so much so that I decided to turn it into a TV programme, called *MasterChef*.

We've come a long way since then. There are now over 60 productions worldwide, and *MasterChef* is seen annually by over 300 million people. I no longer need to defend British food, or any other cuisine, for that matter. The *MasterChef* family has spread all over the globe and the level of cooking that emerges during the competitions is nothing short of breath-taking. Whether it's the Amateurs, the Professionals, the Children or even the Celebrities, many contestants have gone on to open their own restaurants, write their own cookbooks and win Michelin Stars and Chefs' Hats. It is a fantastic validation of *MasterChef*'s role. The cooking in Britain is something to be respected and the chefs in Britain are something to be proud of.

There are new and important challenges ahead of us in the world of food, above and beyond the quality of cooking. We now live in a time where sustainability of produce is in doubt. We also have to consider healthy eating, the health of the soil and the negative effects of food production in an over-populated world. Significantly, we must take a look at the immorality of food waste. These problems must be taken seriously in a way that does not take the pleasure out of eating. It's essential to retain the magic.

The chefs contributing to this book have taken these issues and dealt with them, not as challenges, but as opportunities. The film industry prides itself on being solution-orientated, and the same can be said of chefs. Don't turn your nose up at the idea of healthy eating; you can cook something beautiful and delicious, like Alida Gotta's (Italy) Asparagus with Fried Polenta & Béchamel on page 64, or Gabriel Jonsson's (Sweden) Beetroot and Wheatberry Salad on page 89.

Some of the *MasterChef* challenges have already taken into account the management of waste. The 'Mystery Box' is a great example: what can you make from the produce that is left over from a meal that you have cooked; what can you make with what you find in your fridge? Sowmiya Venkatesan's (Singapore) Spiced Egg Florentine with Paneer on page 40 is out of this world. So, too, is Ana Iglesias Panichelli's (Spain) Courgette 'Spaghetti' with Broccoli Sauce on page 25.

Time is another issue in the modern world. Since the digital revolution we are always on the clock. The computer or mobile phone keeps us alert 24/7; even though they are time-saving devices, they never let us off the hook. We are constantly doing homework. That is why the 'Against the Clock' chapter is a great addition to this book. What can you cook when time is running away from you? Well, try Sandy Tang's (UK) Crispy Tofu Parcels on page 199, or Dino Angelo Luciano's (US) Rice Noodle Fettuccine on page 218. These dishes are quick, healthy and a delight on the eye.

The chapter in the book that means a lot to me, personally, is 'Ordinary to Extraordinary'; this was the notion that inspired me to create *MasterChef*. What can you do with basic produce to turn it into an extraordinary meal? What spicing and flavouring should you add and how should you approach the cooking to make it special? British cooking had, fairly or unfairly, a reputation for spoiling good produce. Not anymore. Take the ordinary and make it extraordinary; see what Thomas Frake (UK) has done with his Sage & Onion Chestnut Roast on page 134. Or Smrutisree Singh (India) with her splendid jackfruit dish on page 114.

Sustainability and the regeneration of the soil will determine the future of the world's crops. Over-farming has caused nutritional depletion in some crops and many of the foods we are eating. They are not giving us the goodness we need and there is also increasing discussion about the growing intolerance to gluten and cows' milk. It's important that we manage the soil and engage with crop rotation. We must cook foods that are healthy for us and keep the planet healthy. Simon Toohey's (Australia) Beetroot Glazed in Soy on page 164 and Lucas Furtado's (Brazil) Mushroom Soup on page 148 are delicious examples of recipes that take full advantage of sustainable crops.

This new *MasterChef* book is modern, thoughtful, inspiring and a gateway into the food of the future. Food that is delicious, healthy and good for the planet.

FRANC RODDAM
Creator of *MasterChef*

introduction

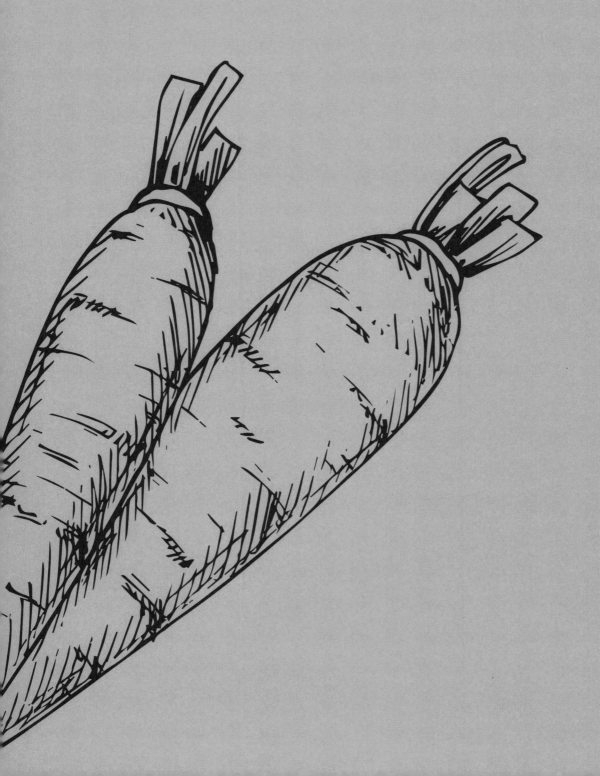

INTRODUCTION

Welcome to *MasterChef Green*, a new and fresh outlook on vegetarian cooking. Here you will find a collection of delicious, modern and creative recipes by myself and *MasterChef* contestants from around the world, all designed to help you expand your knowledge or introduce you to the expansive world of vegetarian cooking. A world of aromatic spices, fresh herbs, protein-rich pulses and joyous moments of seasonality when vegetables and fruit are at their tastiest.

With perceptions towards plant-based eating shifting, there has never been a better time to embrace vegetarianism. For many people, the days of meat forming the focal point on our plates are changing and more vegetable-centric meals are steadily becoming a constant in even the most meat-focused cultures. This is something we can all celebrate for both our physical health and the health of our planet.

Climate change is affecting people across the world, and a major contributor is the farming and consumption of animals. A huge part we can play to help slow down the effects is to consume less meat and dairy. I am by no means telling you to go vegetarian, but the recipes in this book are aimed at giving you exciting skills and tips to help you find joy in vegetable-based food, and even a fully plant-based diet.

Vegetarian cooking is a great opportunity for growth, learning and creativity, all of which *MasterChef* prides itself on. Sometimes you need to think outside the box to bring a dish together with all of the sensory elements that constitute a memorable meal. The Mushroom & Lentil Lasagne on page 176 is a beautiful example of this. The combination of finely diced mushrooms and lentils provides a truly amazing meat-like texture which I'm sure you will be able to cheekily fool many a friend and family member with (I certainly have!).

Another important issue *MasterChef Green* highlights is the importance of reducing food waste by making the absolute most of what we have. To look at ways we can use parts of a vegetable that may often be discarded and turn them into something truly delicious, like the Whole Roasted Cauliflower on page 143, which also uses the cauliflower leaves to make some seriously tasty vegetable crisps, simply by adding just a little sea salt.

This book, with its focus on all things green, would not be complete without talking about sustainability. The word sustainability can mean many things. Not only do you want the ingredients to be sustainably farmed and transported as little as possible, but this is also an opportunity to look at what we are consuming in a broader sense in our lives. How can we return to some traditional methods of both shopping and cooking, and avoid buying ready-made but instead make it ourselves. To learn and create something new in true *MasterChef* style.

For example, recipe in which you make your own pasta and ricotta cheese on page 154 provides a great sense of achievement while also not having to buy something packaged in guilt-inducing single-use plastic.

So whether you are looking for that quick and healthy midweek recipe or a show-stopper of a dish for the weekend with friends and family, I hope this collection of creative, vibrant, nutritious, sustainable and deliciously green recipes will help you embrace or develop a vegetable-led way of cooking and eating.

Adam O'Shepherd
October 2020

mystery
box

I like to think of this bread as one big savoury muffin. As with muffins, you can use whatever ingredients you have to hand to throw into the mix. The courgette can be substituted for other vegetables you may need to use up, so this recipe is really flexible. Using polenta helps to give the loaf added texture and the pickled jalapeños provide a nice little kick.

COURGETTE, SMOKED CHEDDAR & JALAPEÑO BREAD

MAKES 8–10 SLICES

2 courgettes, grated
200g plain flour
100g polenta
2 teaspoons baking powder
1 teaspoon sea salt, plus an
    extra pinch
4 eggs, beaten
150ml milk
75g unsalted butter, melted
1 tablespoon pickled
    jalapeños, chopped
6g coriander, chopped
125g smoked Cheddar, grated
75g vegetarian grating
    cheese, grated

Preheat the oven to 180°C Fan/200°C/Gas Mark 6 and grease and line a 900g loaf tin with baking parchment.

Put the grated courgettes in a clean tea towel with a pinch of salt and give the towel a really hard squeeze a few times to get as much water as you can out of the courgettes.

Combine the flour, polenta, baking powder and 1 teaspoon of salt in a mixing bowl. Add the grated courgettes and mix well.

In another mixing bowl combine the rest of the ingredients. Pour the wet ingredients into the bowl with the flour, polenta and courgettes. Gently fold the mixture together using a spatula. Do not overwork it or the loaf will be tough.

Transfer the batter to the loaf tin, spreading it out evenly using a spatula.

Bake in the hot oven for 45–50 minutes. Check to see if the loaf is done by inserting a skewer into the centre of the loaf. If it comes out clean, it is done. If it's still a little wet, put it back in the oven for another 5 minutes.

Turn the loaf out onto a wire rack and let cool before slicing. Serve toasted for breakfast with Smoky Baked Beans with Wild Mushrooms (see page 99) or Red Pepper Chilli Jam (see page 193).

MasterChef Tip: *Simply slice and serve the bread as it is, or brush both sides of the sliced bread with butter or olive oil, then toast on a hot chargrill pan or in a hot frying pan until golden on both sides.*

These savoury churros are a great way to use up those odd bits of cheese in your fridge. Be adventurous and try different cheese combinations. Serve these as a little pre-dinner party snack or as a canapé for party food. They are also very good with a nice ice-cold beer.

CHEESE CHURROS
WITH SMOKED PAPRIKA MAYO

MAKES ABOUT 25

250ml water
1 tablespoon extra virgin olive oil
1 teaspoon caster sugar
1 teaspoon sea salt flakes, plus
     extra to serve
120g plain flour
1 teaspoon cayenne pepper
30g vegetarian grating cheese,
     grated, plus extra to serve
30g mature Cheddar, grated
sunflower or vegetable oil for
     deep frying

FOR THE SMOKED PAPRIKA MAYO
100g mayonnaise
1 teaspoon smoked paprika
½ tablespoon lemon juice
freshly ground black pepper

To make the churros batter, bring the water and oil to the boil in a saucepan, add the sugar and salt and stir to dissolve. Remove from the heat and gently fold in the flour, cayenne and both of the cheeses then whisk well to combine. Spoon the mixture into a piping bag and refrigerate for at least 30 minutes before using.

Meanwhile, combine the mayonnaise, paprika and lemon juice in a bowl, season with black pepper, then set aside.

If you have a deep-fat fryer, put the oil in it and set the temperature to 180°C. Otherwise, fill a large, heavy-based saucepan one-third full with the sunflower or vegetable oil. Heat until the oil reaches 180°C when tested on a food thermometer. The oil is hot enough when a small piece of bread dropped into it floats to the top and turns golden in 20 seconds.

Take the piping bag from the fridge and begin to pipe the churros into 5–6cm lengths straight into the hot oil. (Take care, as the churros will expand when they hit the hot oil. Wear oven gloves to protect your hands.) Cook the churros for 2–3 minutes until they are nice and golden and floating on the surface. Remove from the oil using a slotted spoon, then drain on kitchen paper. Do not overcrowd the pan as the churros cook – it is best to cook them in 2 batches. After the first batch, leave the oil for 1–2 minutes to come back up to temperature (check using the food thermometer) before cooking the second batch.

Serve the churros with the smoked paprika mayo, extra grated cheese and a sprinkling of sea salt flakes.

Broths really sing of seasonality, and they're ideal for making the most of what's fresh, abundant and locally grown. A good broth provides comfort and warmth, whether you're sharing with others now, or storing leftovers for a freezer stash when you're on your own. Pearl barley has the most wonderful chewy texture and has the added benefit of soaking up all of the flavours in the broth. Use a variety of vegetables depending on what you have to hand. The saffron mayonnaise makes this broth that little bit more special, and it's certain not to disappoint.

PEARL BARLEY BROTH
WITH CAVOLO NERO & SAFFRON MAYO

SERVES 4

2 tablespoons olive oil
1 brown onion, finely chopped
1 celery stick, finely chopped
1 small carrot, finely chopped
½ teaspoon chilli flakes
2 garlic cloves, finely chopped
1 teaspoon thyme leaves
150g pearl barley
1.5 litres hot vegetable stock,
  plus extra if needed
150g frozen peas, defrosted
250g cavolo nero, leaves
  chopped and stalks finely
  chopped
zest of ½ lemon
sea salt and freshly ground
  black pepper

FOR THE SAFFRON MAYO
pinch of saffron threads
5 tablespoons mayonnaise
½ tablespoon lemon juice
sea salt and freshly ground
  black pepper

TO SERVE
2 tablespoons finely chopped
  flat-leaf parsley
sourdough slices, toasted

Heat the olive oil in a large saucepan over a medium heat then add the onion, celery and carrot and a pinch of sea salt. Cook, stirring, until the vegetables are soft but not browned, for about 5 minutes. Add the chilli flakes, garlic and thyme leaves and cook for 1 minute more.

Add the pearl barley and stir to coat with the vegetable mixture for 1 minute then add the hot vegetable stock. Bring to the boil, reduce the heat to low and simmer for 20 minutes until the pearl barley is tender. Season as necessary.

While the broth is simmering, mix the ingredients for the saffron mayo in a small bowl and set aside. Season if needed.

Add the defrosted peas to the broth followed by the cavolo nero and lemon zest. Cook for 1–2 minutes to wilt the cavolo nero. Serve ladled into 4 bowls, sprinkled with a little salt, the chopped parsley, a dollop of the saffron mayonnaise and the sourdough on the side.

Soups bring endless possibilities and don't take a great deal of planning – just scan the fridge, freezer or pantry to see what you have on hand. Don't be afraid to experiment a bit, as new combinations often yield the most exciting results. This is a lovely light soup, summery with the freshness of sweetcorn, cherry tomatoes and a little punch of heat from chilli and canned poblano peppers.

TOMATO & POBLANO PEPPER NOODLE SOUP

SERVES 4

100g rice noodles
2 tablespoons olive oil
1 small brown onion, finely
    chopped
1 garlic clove, finely chopped
1 green chilli, deseeded and
    chopped
1 teaspoon ground coriander
1 teaspoon ground cumin
8 cherry tomatoes, halved
1 litre vegetable stock
3 poblano peppers from a jar
    (or 2 roasted green peppers),
    drained, deseeded and cut
    into 0.5cm strips
4 tablespoons sweetcorn
    kernels (canned, fresh or
    frozen, defrosted)
juice of 1 lime
sea salt and freshly ground
    black pepper

TO SERVE
toasted pumpkin seeds
chopped coriander
soured cream
chopped chillies (optional)
hot sauce (optional)

Cook the rice noodles for a minute less than the packet instructions, drain and set aside.

In a large saucepan, heat the olive oil and cook the onion, garlic and chilli over a low heat for 2–3 minutes, stirring, until they are soft. Add the ground coriander and cumin and cook for a further 30 seconds then add the cherry tomatoes and vegetable stock.

Bring to the boil and add the peppers and sweetcorn. Reduce the heat to low-medium and cook for 15–20 minutes. Season with lime juice, salt and pepper.

Serve the noodles in bowls, then ladle over the soup. Sprinkle with the pumpkin seeds and coriander and serve with soured cream.

For those who like it really spicy, some freshly chopped chilli or a bottle of hot sauce will always hit the spot.

Pulses and grains are so versatile. Having a good assortment of both in your pantry will provide a good base that you can quickly build a soup upon. While fresh vegetables bring freshness and colour, pulses and grains give a soup body and depth, turning something light into a hearty and substantial meal.

CHICKPEA, KALE & FREEKEH SOUP
WITH LABNEH

SERVES 4

200g freekeh (cracked wheat)
2 tablespoons olive oil
1 medium onion, finely chopped
1 medium carrot, finely chopped
2 garlic cloves, finely chopped
1 teaspoon ground cumin
1 teaspoon ground coriander
1 teaspoon dried oregano
2 litres vegetable stock, hot
100g kale, shredded
400g can chickpeas, drained
1 teaspoon sumac
crusty bread to serve (optional)
sea salt and freshly ground
    black pepper

FOR THE LABNEH
360g full-fat Greek yogurt

Begin by making the labneh. Put the yogurt in a clean piece of muslin and add a pinch of sea salt. Tie the muslin securely, put it in a fine sieve and position it over a large bowl or deep pan to catch the liquid. Transfer to the fridge and leave overnight or for at least 6 hours. The labneh is ready when it has a firm texture.

Rinse the freekeh a few times under cold water and set aside.

Heat the olive oil in a large saucepan (use one with a lid) over a medium heat, add the onion and carrot and cook, stirring, until soft, about 5 minutes. Add the garlic and cook for a further minute. Add the cumin, coriander and oregano and cook for 30 seconds to release their aromas.

Add the freekeh and stock, give it a stir and, once it has come to the boil, reduce to a simmer, cover with the lid and simmer for 20 minutes.

Once the freekeh is tender, add the kale and chickpeas and cook for another 5 minutes. Taste and season with salt and pepper. Serve in bowls topped with a heaped dessertspoon of labneh and sprinkled with the sumac, with some crusty bread on the side.

ANA IGLESIAS PANICHELLI MASTERCHEF SPAIN CHAMPION 2020

Saying I love pasta is an understatement. Luckily for me, I've been introduced to the wonders of courgette 'pasta'. Twice the nutrients and fewer calories: that's a clear win-win. So, if you're trying to find balance in your pasta intake, then you'll love this dish. To keep it green and tasty, we'll pair it with the creamiest broccoli sauce.

A spiralizer will come in handy for this recipe, but if you don't have one you can always improvise and make noodle-like zucchini strands using a mandoline or by slicing it thinly into spaghetti-like strips using a sharp knife.

This is a great recipe for using up those odds and ends from the fridge, such as an overabundance of courgettes, or too much blue cheese. Turn your leftovers into a delicious dish.

COURGETTE 'SPAGHETTI'
WITH BROCCOLI SAUCE

SERVES 2

1 tablespoon extra virgin olive oil
2 garlic cloves, crushed
2 courgettes, sliced into thin, spaghetti-like strands (see introduction, above)

FOR THE BROCCOLI SAUCE

1 whole broccoli, cut into 4cm pieces
1 tablespoon extra virgin olive oil
1 onion, chopped
220g soured cream
25g blue cheese (check it's vegetarian)
1 teaspoon salt
½ teaspoon pepper
1 teaspoon freshly grated nutmeg
1 teaspoon mixed seeds, to serve (optional)

To make the broccoli sauce, bring a saucepan of water to the boil, add the broccoli pieces and boil for about 6–8 minutes, until tender.

Meanwhile, in a separate saucepan, heat the olive oil over a medium heat, add the onion then cook, stirring frequently, until softened. When the broccoli is tender, drain it in a colander then add the drained broccoli to the pan with the onion and cook, stirring.

After 2–3 minutes add the soured cream and blue cheese and stir well to melt the cheese and to reduce the sauce, about 4 minutes. When the sauce is reduced, season with the salt, pepper and nutmeg.

At this stage, you can either blend the sauce using a stick blender for a smoother consistency or leave it chunky, as you prefer.

For the courgette spaghetti, heat the olive oil in a large frying pan over a medium heat, add the garlic cloves and cook, stirring frequently, for about 2–3 minutes (don't let the garlic burn).

Add the courgette spaghetti and cook, stirring occasionally, for 7 minutes until crisp. Add the broccoli sauce and stir gently to mix. Garnish with mixed seeds, if you like, and enjoy!

Polenta is a great pantry staple to use in savoury and sweet dishes. Sicilian caponata has a wonderful savoury-sweet balance, which comes from slow-cooked caramelised aubergine, capers and sweet currants. Traditionally caponata is served with crusty bread but with polenta alongside it makes a gorgeous light lunch or starter. This is a recipe that's worth making in larger batches for the freezer.

POLENTA
WITH CAPONATA & GRIDDLED GEM LETTUCE

SERVES 4

olive oil, to grease, plus extra
   to drizzle
1 litre vegetable stock
150g polenta
40g vegetarian grating cheese,
   grated
20g unsalted butter
sea salt and freshly ground
   black pepper

FOR THE CAPONATA
50ml olive oil
2 aubergines, cut into 1cm pieces
1 brown onion, chopped
2 garlic cloves, finely chopped
2 large ripe tomatoes, chopped
20g currants
2 teaspoons capers, chopped
25ml red wine vinegar

FOR THE GRIDDLED GEM LETTUCE
2 tablespoons olive oil
2 gem lettuces, halved

TO SERVE
2 tablespoons toasted pine nuts
8 basil leaves, torn

Grease a shallow baking tray with a little olive oil and line with baking parchment.

For the polenta, bring the vegetable stock to the boil in a saucepan, then reduce to a simmer. Add the polenta gradually, whisking constantly until all of the polenta is combined with the stock. Using a wooden spoon, keep stirring the polenta for another 2 minutes, making sure it is smooth.

Take the polenta off the heat and add 25g of the grated cheese and the butter and season with salt and pepper. Pour the polenta into the prepared tray, spreading it out evenly. Allow the polenta to cool then transfer to the fridge for 2–3 hours, ideally overnight.

For the caponata, heat 2½ tablespoons of the olive oil in a saucepan over a medium heat, then add the aubergine. Cook for 15 minutes until the pieces are broken down and nice and caramelised. Using a spoon, scoop out the aubergine and set aside.

In the same saucepan, cook the onion and garlic in the remaining oil. Cook for 2–3 minutes until soft. Add the tomatoes and cook for another 5 minutes until they start to break down. Add the currants, capers and vinegar then simmer on the lowest heat for 20 minutes. Stir the aubergine back in and season, if necessary, then leave the caponata to rest for 10–15 minutes before serving.

Preheat the oven to 200°C Fan/180°C/Gas Mark 6.

Remove the polenta from the fridge and cut into 8 rectangular pieces. Put the polenta onto a clean baking tray lined with parchment paper, drizzle with a little extra olive oil and sprinkle over the remaining 1 tablespoon grated cheese. Bake for 10–15 minutes until nice and crisp.

While the polenta is baking, heat a frying pan over a high heat with the 2 tablespoons olive oil and cook the lettuce for 2 minutes on each side until nice and golden and slightly charred. Season with sea salt and cracked pepper.

To serve, put the polenta rectangles onto plates. Spoon a good amount of the caponata over half of the polenta, top with the pine nuts and basil leaves and serve with a wedge of the griddled gem lettuce alongside.

These rolls say sun, warmth and vitality. Rice paper rolls are lovely filled with prawns, but smoked tofu (something I recommend always having on hand) mirrors their texture and is packed full of flavour. Don't be shy to load them up with the crunchy satay sauce.

SUMMER ROLLS
WITH SMOKED TOFU & SATAY SAUCE

MAKES 6 ROLLS

50g rice noodles
6 x 22cm rice paper sheets
150g smoked tofu, cut into
    12 thin slices
⅓ cucumber, seeds removed
    and julienned
1 medium carrot, julienned
12g mint, leaves picked and torn
12g coriander, leaves picked

FOR THE SATAY SAUCE
1 tablespoon sunflower oil
2 shallots, finely chopped
2 garlic cloves, finely chopped
15g ginger, peeled and grated
1 stalk lemongrass, finely
    chopped
1 red chilli, finely chopped
150ml coconut milk
50ml water
1 tablespoon soy sauce
½ tablespoon kecap manis
½ tablespoon rice vinegar
80g crunchy peanut butter
pinch of sea salt (optional)

To make the satay sauce, heat the sunflower oil in a saucepan over a medium heat. When hot, add the shallots, garlic, ginger, lemongrass and chilli then cook, stirring, for 2–3 minutes.

Add the coconut milk, water, soy sauce, kecap manis and vinegar and bring to the boil. Add the peanut butter then turn the heat to low and simmer the satay sauce for 5–10 minutes. Taste to see if the satay needs salt and add a pinch if need be. If the satay looks too thick, add a little more water.

Cook the rice noodles according to the packet instructions, drain and set aside. Splash a little cold water over the noodles to prevent them sticking while you prepare the summer rolls.

Fill a bowl (use one wide enough to fit the rice paper sheets) with hot water. Sit a small bowl of water next to you for dipping your fingers into. Take one rice paper sheet at a time and dip it in the water then wait for the paper to soften for 10 seconds. Remove from the water and place flat on a clean work surface.

Arrange rice noodles down the centre of the paper, leaving 1cm at either side. Add 2 pieces of the smoked tofu followed by cucumber, carrot and a few leaves of mint and coriander.

Dip your fingers into the bowl of water (rolling will be easier with wet fingers). Roll the rice paper sheet halfway up to encase the filling then tuck in the ends to enclose and finish rolling the rice paper sheet the rest of the way.

Repeat the process with the other rolls. Cut each roll in half and serve on a platter with a bowl of the satay sauce.

See pages 28–29 for the recipe photograph.

Piping hot mac 'n' cheese fresh out of the oven is a sight to behold. The bubbling cheese sauce trying to make its way through the golden crusted topping never fails to set the taste buds alight. It's also an opportunity to get creative. Use fresh herbs and salad leaves in the white sauce and add some nuts for added texture. Yes, it's quite literally green, and will be a great hit with humans of all ages.

GREEN MAC 'N' CHEESE
WITH AN ALMOND CRUMB

SERVES 4–5

350g macaroni
100g sourdough, torn into pieces
30g blanched almonds
50g butter
1 small brown onion, chopped
2 garlic cloves, finely chopped
30g plain flour
700ml milk
100g mature Cheddar, grated
½ tablespoon Dijon mustard
1 teaspoon thyme leaves
65g vegetarian grating cheese, grated
150g frozen peas, defrosted
30g baby spinach
6g flat-leaf parsley, leaves picked
6g basil leaves
sea salt and freshly ground black pepper

Preheat the oven to 180°C Fan/200°C/Gas Mark 6.

Cook the macaroni in boiling salted water for 2 minutes less than the instructions on the packet, then drain under cold water to stop the pasta cooking further.

Whizz the sourdough and almonds in a food processor until a smallish crumb forms, then set aside.

Heat the butter in a large saucepan over a medium heat and cook the onion and garlic for 2 minutes until soft, stirring. Add the flour and cook, stirring, for a minute until a paste forms. Gradually add 600ml of the milk, using a whisk to create a smooth white sauce.

Turn the heat down to low and let simmer for 3–5 minutes until the sauce has thickened slightly, then season with salt and cracked black pepper. Off the heat, stir in the Cheddar, Dijon mustard, thyme, 50g of the vegetarian grating cheese and the peas.

Whizz the remaining 100ml milk in a blender with the spinach, parsley and basil and add this mixture to the white sauce. Fold in the macaroni and mix well to combine. Pour the green mac 'n' cheese into a 24 x 18cm baking dish and top with the almond crumb and remaining vegetarian grating cheese.

Bake in the oven for 25 minutes until the crumb topping is golden and the mac 'n' cheese is bubbling. Leave to rest for 10 minutes before serving.

Serve with a few crisp salad leaves simply dressed with good oil and a little lemon juice.

See pages 32–33 for the recipe photograph.

It is a useful skill and a real joy to be able to rummage through the cupboards and get creative using what you find there. Use store cupboard staples like canned pulses to add weight to a salad. Think about how you can use the whole vegetable with all of its stalks and leaves, which will provide extra nutrients and limit food waste. Crusty old bits of bread lying around? They can be turned into little crumbs of textural happiness.

PUY LENTIL SALAD
WITH CHARRED TENDERSTEM BROCCOLI, PANGRATTATO & MISO DRESSING

SERVES 2

200g canned puy (French) lentils
1 shallot, very finely chopped
1 tablespoon balsamic vinegar
1 tablespoon olive oil
1 tablespoon lemon juice
1 tablespoon finely chopped flat-leaf parsley
150g tenderstem broccoli, halved lengthways, using entire stalk and leaves
sea salt and freshly ground black pepper

FOR THE PANGRATTATO

100g stale bread, roughly torn into small pieces
1 tablespoon grated vegetarian grating cheese
pinch of chilli flakes
1 teaspoon chopped rosemary leaves
½ garlic clove, grated
1½ tablespoons olive oil

FOR THE MISO DRESSING

60ml olive oil
juice of ¼ lemon
20g miso paste
1 garlic clove, finely chopped

Preheat the oven to 160°C Fan/180°C/Gas Mark 4. Mix all of the pangrattato ingredients in a bowl then spread out on a baking tray and bake for 10–12 minutes until crunchy. Set aside and leave to cool.

Mix all the ingredients for the miso dressing in a separate bowl and set aside.

Put the lentils and shallot in a separate large bowl and dress with the balsamic, oil and lemon juice then add the parsley. Season with sea salt and cracked black pepper. Spoon the lentils on to 2 plates or shallow bowls.

Heat a frying pan over a high heat. When hot, add the broccoli. Try not to move it around for a minute or so to let it char slightly. Add the miso dressing to the pan and cook, stirring, for a further minute.

Serve the broccoli on top of the lentils with the pangrattato sprinkled over the top.

Making a savoury tart is the perfect way to use up last-leg veg, and there's no limit to combinations for the filling. Mix things up by using different cheeses, wilting salad leaves and herbs, or even toss in the leftover roast veggies from last night's dinner. The twist of using spelt flour for the pastry results in a tart with a lovely, nutty, wholesome exterior.

LEEK, CHEESE & ROCKET SPELT-CRUSTED TART

SERVES 4–6

150g spelt flour
100g plain flour, plus extra
   for dusting
1 teaspoon sea salt
125g cold unsalted butter, diced
4 tablespoons cold water
1 egg, beaten

FOR THE FILLING

2 tablespoons olive oil
3 small leeks, washed and
   thinly sliced
4 eggs, beaten
250ml double cream
100ml crème fraîche
40g vegetarian grating cheese,
   grated
50g rocket
1 tablespoon pumpkin seeds
sea salt and freshly ground
   black pepper

Preheat the oven to 170°C Fan/190°C/Gas Mark 5.

Make the pastry in a food processor. Put both flours and the salt in the bowl of the food processor and, with the motor running, add the diced cold butter and process until rough crumbs begin to form. Add the cold water 1 tablespoon at a time until it forms a smooth dough. Wrap the dough in baking parchment or beeswax cotton wrap and chill in the fridge for 30 minutes.

On a lightly floured work surface, roll out the pastry so it is smooth and flat, to a 2–3mm thickness. Put the pastry in a 20cm loose-bottomed tart tin and work it into the edges so that it is nice and flush up against the sides of the tin. Trim off any excess pastry (save it for another recipe or freeze it). Chill the tart case in the fridge for 10 minutes.

Line the tart case with baking parchment, fill it with ceramic baking beans or raw rice then blind-bake the pastry case for 15 minutes. Remove the ceramic baking beans and parchment, brush the pastry with the beaten egg and put the case back in the oven for another 10 minutes until nice and golden.

While the tart case is baking, prepare the filling. Heat the oil in a pan over a medium-low heat and cook the leeks, stirring, for 10 minutes, adding a pinch of salt. Stir regularly to prevent them from colouring. They just need to be lovely and tender and soft. Remove from the heat and cool.

In a mixing bowl, combine the eggs, cream, crème fraîche, grated cheese and rocket and season with salt and pepper. Add the leeks, stir well, then pour into the prepared pastry case. Sprinkle the pumpkin seeds over the top and bake for 35 minutes until it has set.

Leave to cool for 10–15 minutes before serving. Serve warm or cold.

This is a recipe for those days when you're thinking, 'What do I have on hand to whip up?' Grab some canned pulses and dried spices from the pantry, then it's just a case of adding a little creativity. This pie is certainly big on flavour. The spices bring warmth while the potato topping gives it sweetness.

SPICED CHICKPEA & SWEET POTATO PIE

SERVES 4–6

600g sweet potatoes, peeled
   and cut into 4cm chunks
250g Maris Piper potatoes,
   peeled and cut into
   4cm chunks
2 spring onions, finely chopped
80g unsalted butter, diced
2 tablespoons olive oil
2 small red onions, diced into
   0.5cm pieces
1 medium carrot, diced into
   0.5cm pieces
2 celery sticks, diced into
   0.5cm pieces
2 garlic cloves, finely chopped
150g chestnut mushrooms,
   quartered
1 teaspoon ground cinnamon
1 teaspoon ground cumin
1 teaspoon ground coriander
½ teaspoon ground turmeric
½ teaspoon chilli flakes
400g can chopped tomatoes
250ml vegetable stock
2 x 400g cans chickpeas, drained
150g baby spinach
sea salt and freshly ground
   black pepper

Preheat the oven to 180°C Fan/200°C/Gas Mark 6.

Bring a saucepan of water to the boil and cook the sweet potato and potato chunks until they are soft enough to pierce easily with the top of a knife. Drain well then put a clean tea towel over the colander holding the sweet potatoes/potatoes and leave for 5 minutes to help them dry.

Return the sweet potatoes/potatoes to the saucepan along with the spring onions and butter, then mash well. Season with salt and pepper and set aside.

Heat the olive oil in a separate saucepan over a medium heat and cook the onion, carrot and celery, stirring, for 5–7 minutes until they begin to soften. Add the garlic and mushrooms and cook for another 2 minutes. Add the cinnamon, cumin, coriander, turmeric and chilli flakes and cook, stirring, to coat the vegetables.

Add the tomatoes and vegetable stock to the pan and bring to the boil. Reduce the heat to medium and cook for 20 minutes until thickened. Add the chickpeas and baby spinach and cook for another 1–2 minutes to wilt the spinach.

Spoon the pie filling into a 24 x 18cm baking tin and carefully top with the mashed sweet potato/potato. Bake in the oven for 25–30 minutes until the mash topping is crispy in parts. Leave the pie to rest for 10–15 minutes before serving with seasonal sautéed greens.

MasterChef Tip: **If you are feeling indulgent you could also add a little grated cheese to the topping 5–10 minutes before the pie comes out of the oven.**

Green leftovers in your fridge have short lifespans. Well past their salad heydays, they lurk and threaten to wilt. But with a little imagination, there are many delectable dishes you can conjure up to rescue them. This super-simple meal can pass for breakfast, lunch or dinner. It's easy on the cooking skills and it ticks all the boxes on eating healthily (even if the ingredients are not in their prime). Feel free to replace the block of paneer with tofu or halloumi cheese. As long as you have a hot pan to sear, you are good.

SPICED EGG FLORENTINE
WITH PANEER

SERVES 1

leftover greens and herbs,
    torn into even pieces
1 tablespoon ghee
½ red onion, finely chopped
½ teaspoon ginger-garlic-green
    chilli paste (see recipe below)
¼ teaspoon ground cumin
pinch of sugar
½ teaspoon lemon juice
Himalayan pink salt

FOR THE GINGER-GARLIC-GREEN
    CHILLI PASTE (MAKES ENOUGH
    FOR 4–5 PEOPLE)
1cm piece ginger, peeled and
    roughly chopped
12 garlic cloves, roughly chopped
3 green chillies, roughly chopped
    (keep or discard the seeds
    depending on how spicy you
    like your food)
3 tablespoons vegetable oil

FOR THE PANEER
225g pack paneer
2 teaspoons ghee

FOR THE POACHED EGG
1 egg (cold from the fridge)

Start with the chilli paste. Whizz the ingredients to a paste in a mini food processor. This recipe will make more than you need , but you can use it in so many Indian recipes. Just transfer the excess to an airtight jar and store in the fridge for up to 2 weeks.

Let's do the paneer. Lay a sheet of kitchen paper on a work surface, place the paneer on it and pat it dry. Using a 9cm round cookie cutter, carefully cut the paneer into a disc. (Save the leftover paneer for another recipe.)

Heat the a frying pan over a high heat. When it's hot, add the paneer disc – it should sizzle just like a steak. Sear for 2 minutes on each side, turning carefully. Add the ghee and tilt the pan from side to side, so the melted ghee helps to sear the paneer all over. Paneer can burn easily so the process should not take more than 5 minutes. Remove the paneer disc from the heat and drain on kitchen paper. Keep the pan for the greens and the tempering.

To poach the egg, fill a saucepan with 10cm of water and bring it to a boil. Add an additional 1cm of cool or room temperature water to the boiling water – the water should no longer be boiling (the temperature then should be 75°C/167°F).

Slowly lower the egg into the water and set a timer for 12 minutes. Fill another bowl with ice cubes and water to make an ice bath. As soon as the timer goes off, quickly remove the egg using a slotted spoon and gently lower it into the ice bath. Let it sit there for 1 minute, then transfer to a plate and set aside.

Meanwhile, rinse the leftover greens and herbs in a colander and leave to drain. Heat the ghee in the frying pan on a low to medium heat. Add the chopped onion and let it cook slowly until it is translucent. Add the ginger-garlic-green chilli paste to the pan, stir for 1 minute, then add the ground cumin. Cook, stirring, until the raw smell of the ginger-garlic-green chill is gone, typically 30 seconds to 1 minute.

FOR THE TEMPERING
1 tablespoon ghee
½ teaspoon cumin seeds

TO GARNISH
¼ teaspoon ground cumin
**¼ teaspoon Kashmiri
  chilli powder**
**¼ teaspoon chaat masala
  spice mix**

Increase the heat to high, quickly add the greens and toss them around in the pan. Season with salt and a pinch of sugar then turn off the heat. Add the lemon juice, mix well, then tip the cooked greens into a colander to drain away the liquid until you are ready to serve.

For the tempering, use the same pan you used for the paneer and heat it over a high heat. Add the ghee and, when melted, add the cumin seeds and let them splutter (but don't let them burn). Remove from the heat.

To serve, put the paneer disc on a plate then stack the greens on top. Use a spoon to make a small indentation in the greens. Nestle the poached egg on top of the greens.

Garnish with the ghee and cumin tempering, sprinkle over the ground cumin, Kashmiri chilli powder, chaat masala and Himalayan pink salt, to taste, and enjoy.

Vegetarian burgers incite debate. What constitutes a good one? What sets a good one apart from a brilliant one? A good veggie burger should have a robust texture – a mushy patty in a soft bun can be quite the let-down. Grains and pulses from the store cupboard are ideal for providing that texture, so have some fun experimenting with different grains (brown rice works well). I like to start with mushrooms, which provide a meaty texture, for the main part of the patty and build from there.

THE 'QUARTER POUNDER' BURGER

SERVES 6

100g freekeh (cracked wheat)
3 tablespoons olive oil
250g portobello mushrooms,
  very finely chopped
4 thyme sprigs, leaves picked
1 teaspoon dried oregano
1 teaspoon smoked paprika
400g can haricot beans, drained
  and rinsed
2 garlic cloves, roughly chopped
2 tablespoons soy sauce
70g panko breadcrumbs
1 egg, beaten
80g smoked cheese, sliced
80g Cheddar, sliced
sea salt and freshly ground
  black pepper

FOR THE QUICK PICKLE
⅓ cucumber, thinly sliced
½ brown onion, thinly sliced
1 tablespoon rice vinegar
good pinch each of sea salt
  and caster sugar

TO SERVE
6 brioche burger buns
tomato ketchup

Rinse the freekeh well under cold water then drain. Cook the freekeh in a pan of salted water for 25 minutes over a medium heat until it is tender but still has a little bite to it. Drain and leave to cool.

Heat the olive oil in a frying pan over a medium heat and add the mushrooms with the thyme, oregano, smoked paprika and a little salt. Cook, stirring, for 5–7 minutes until the mushrooms are starting to crisp up and all of the oil has been absorbed. Remove from the heat and leave to cool.

Blend the haricot beans in a food processor with the garlic and soy sauce.

Combine the blended bean mix, freekeh and mushrooms in a mixing bowl. Add the breadcrumbs, and egg, mix well to combine, then season well with salt and pepper. Shape the mixture into 6 evenly sized patties, put on a baking tray lined with baking parchment and chill in the fridge for 45 minutes to an hour to firm up.

While the patties are chilling, put the cucumber and onion for the quick pickle in a glass or ceramic bowl and add the vinegar, salt and sugar. Use your hands to give the mixture a gentle squeeze, then leave to pickle for 15–20 minutes.

Preheat the oven to 180°C Fan/200°C/Gas Mark 6.

Remove the patties from the fridge, transfer to the hot oven and cook for 15–20 minutes until they have formed a nice crust on them. Top the patties with equal quantities of the cheeses and return to the oven for 2–3 minutes to melt the cheese.

Set the patties aside to rest while you toast the brioche buns.

Serve the patties on the toasted buns, with a small amount of ketchup, and some pickle.

Ready-rolled puff pastry tucked away in the freezer is a useful pantry item, and can be the simple solution to a quick-fix, no-planning meal. This comforting and delicious pie is super-easy to make and can be adapted using other seasonal root vegetables or pulses too.

SWEET POTATO, ONION & EMMENTAL PIE

SERVES 6

600g sweet potatoes, peeled and diced into 2cm pieces
3 small red onions, peeled and quartered
3 tablespoons olive oil
butter, for greasing
640g puff pastry (2 ready rolled sheets)
150g spring greens, chopped
juice of ¼ lemon
6 sage leaves, finely sliced
100g Emmental, grated (check the label to make sure it's vegetarian)
1 egg, beaten
sea salt and freshly ground black pepper

Preheat the oven to 180°C Fan/200°C/Gas Mark 6.

Put the sweet potato on one baking tray and the onions on another. Drizzle a tablespoon of olive oil over each, transfer to the oven and roast the sweet potato for 25 minutes and the onions for 15 minutes.

Grease a 20cm loose-bottomed tart tin with butter and unroll one of the pastry sheets onto it, tucking it into the edges. Trim the edges around the tart tin, then chill in the fridge for 15 minutes. (Keep the pastry offcuts for another dish; wrap well and freeze for up to 3 months.)

Heat the remaining tablespoon of olive oil in a frying pan, add the spring greens and cook, stirring, over a medium heat for 2–3 minutes, then set aside.

When the sweet potato and onions have finished roasting, put both in a mixing bowl along with the spring greens. Add the lemon juice, sage and the cheese. Mix well and season with salt and pepper.

Remove the tart case from the fridge and spread the pie filling evenly over the base using a spoon or spatula. Unroll the second piece of puff pastry and place it over the top. Press the edges of both pastry sheets together to form a seal, then trim the edges (see tip below about offcuts).

Using a pastry brush, brush the pie lid well with the beaten egg. Scatter sea salt flakes and a little freshly cracked black pepper over the top. Bake in the oven for 40–45 minutes until you have wonderfully crisp and golden pastry. Leave the pie to stand for 10–15 minutes before serving with seasonal sautéed greens.

MasterChef Tip: *To use up odds and ends of leftover pastry, make quick Danish-style pastries: roll out into small squares, put some mashed fruit in the centre and roll the edges inwards before baking until golden for 15 or so minutes. Or, roll the pastry back into a ball, wrap well and freeze for later use.*

healthy
eating

A platter of nibbles is a simple, effortless way of sharing with others. Partner it with some good wine and good conversation, and you can't ask for much more from life. The beauty of a sharing platter is that there are no rules about what to include — have whatever your taste buds feel like.

GRILLED VEGETABLES
WITH BUTTERBEAN HUMMUS, OLIVES & PITTA BREAD

SERVES 4

**2 small courgettes, cut into
5cm lengths**
**2 red peppers, deseeded and
cut into 2cm strips**
olive oil, for brushing
**1 portion Butterbean Hummus
(see page 185)**
**80g olives (nocellara or other
green olives)**
**small handful picked
parsley leaves**
extra virgin olive oil, for drizzling
sumac, for sprinkling
sea salt

TO SERVE
6 pittas, toasted
lemon wedges

Heat a ridged grill pan over a high heat. Brush the courgettes and peppers with olive oil and place in the grill pan, working in batches. Sprinkle the vegetables with sea salt and cook until they're soft and tender with some nice charred marks (around 5 minutes), turning the vegetables regularly.

Spread the hummus over the base of a serving platter then layer over the grilled courgettes and red peppers along with the olives. Arrange the parsley on top, drizzle over extra virgin olive oil and sprinkle with sumac.

Serve with toasted pittas and lemon wedges.

See pages 50–51 for the recipe photograph.

Pearl barley tops my list of grains to use in salads. This mighty grain packs more of a nutritional punch than white rice, for example, as it is high in fibre. It has contrasting textures – a slight bite and a soft chewiness – and it soaks up flavours wonderfully. This is a great autumnal salad. It's comforting, filling and has the added benefit of vitamin C to help keep the immune system healthy in the colder months.

ARTICHOKE, ORANGE & PEARL BARLEY SALAD

SERVES 4

280g pearl barley
olive oil, for frying
200g marinated artichokes, drained
3 oranges, peeled and segmented
4 small red chicory, leaves separated and halved
50g watercress
small handful basil leaves, torn
2 tablespoons almonds, toasted and roughly chopped

FOR THE BALSAMIC DRESSING
100ml extra virgin olive oil
50ml balsamic vinegar
1 tablespoon Dijon mustard
1 tablespoon lemon juice
sea salt and freshly ground black pepper

Bring a saucepan of salted water to the boil and cook the pearl barley over a medium heat for 25–30 minutes, or until tender. Drain well and set aside to cool.

Heat a little olive oil in a frying pan and fry the drained artichokes for 2–3 minutes to crisp them up a little.

To make the dressing, whisk the olive oil, balsamic, mustard and lemon juice together in a bowl. Season with salt and pepper and set aside.

Once the pearl barley has cooled, combine it in a mixing bowl with the artichokes, orange segments, chicory, watercress and basil. Dress with the balsamic dressing and scatter the almonds over the top.

MasterChef Tip: *To save yourself time during the week, you can batch-cook grains and pulses for your other dishes. Try cooking extra pearl barley to use as a base for a lovely risotto or to add to a hearty soup.*

See pages 54–55 for the recipe photograph.

This is a salad to really awaken the senses. The kimchi provides the spicy, salty and sweet elements, the red grapefruit brings sourness, and the cucumber and cashews provide the salad-y crunch. The kimchi helps deliver good bacteria to the digestive system and the red grapefruit is high in antioxidants.

GRAPEFRUIT, KIMCHI & CUCUMBER SALAD

SERVES 4

2 red grapefruit, peeled and
   segmented
300g Kimchi (see page 63),
   roughly chopped
½ cucumber, cut into
   small chunks
250g beansprouts
1 tablespoon sriracha hot sauce
juice of ½ lime
12g coriander, leaves picked
12g Thai basil, leaves
   roughly torn
4 tablespoons cashews, toasted
   and roughly chopped
sea salt

Combine the grapefruit, kimchi, cucumber, beansprouts, sriracha and lime juice in a mixing bowl and leave to rest for 5 minutes to let the flavour from the kimchi absorb into the salad.

Gently fold in the coriander, Thai basil and half the cashews. Gently mix the salad and season with a little salt, taking care not to bruise the herbs. Serve in bowls, scattered with the rest of the cashews.

The classic potato salad, the sort many of us have grown up with and eaten at summer barbecues, gets a little makeover. This is a healthier, fresher and more fragrant version. I am a big fan of fruit in salads, and the apple pairs really well with the earthiness of the potato and celeriac. The yogurt, soured cream and dill give it an edgy zing.

CELERIAC, APPLE & POTATO SALAD
WITH DILL & MUSTARD DRESSING

SERVES 2 AS A MAIN, 4 AS A SIDE

250g new potatoes, halved (skin left on)
200g celeriac, grated
1 Granny Smith apple, peeled, cored and cut into matchsticks
½ red onion, finely sliced
1 tablespoon sunflower seeds, toasted
handful rocket or watercress leaves

FOR THE DRESSING
120ml soured cream
60ml mayonnaise
60ml natural yogurt
½ tablespoon Dijon mustard
1 tablespoon lemon juice
2 tablespoons finely chopped dill
sea salt and freshly ground black pepper

Put the new potatoes in a saucepan of salted water and bring to the boil. Simmer for 10–12 minutes until tender. Drain the potatoes, return them to the pan, then leave them to cool with a clean tea towel over them to draw out any excess moisture.

Combine all of the salad dressing ingredients in a bowl, mix well and season with salt and pepper.

Combine the potatoes, celeriac, apple, onion and sunflower seeds in a large bowl. Add the dressing and toss to combine. Gently fold in half of the rocket or watercress then serve the salad with the remaining leaves scattered over the top.

This salad is a great example of using fresh produce at its seasonal best. Tomatoes and fennel are both brimming with flavour in the summer months, and perfectly timed for salad season. Fennel is lovely and sharp with an aniseedy flavour when eaten raw, but when it's roasted its sweetness comes to life. Fennel is a good source of vitamin C, and sherry vinegar can provide 'good' bacteria to help improve gut health.

TOMATO & ROAST FENNEL SALAD
WITH CAPERS & SHERRY VINEGAR

SERVES 4

2 fennel bulbs, roughly chopped
3 tablespoons olive oil
2 large slices sourdough, torn
　　into 2cm pieces
4 large vine tomatoes, roughly
　　chopped
2 tablespoons capers, drained
1 tablespoon lemon juice
1 tablespoon sherry vinegar
3 tablespoons extra virgin
　　olive oil
30g rocket
handful basil leaves, torn
sea salt and freshly ground
　　black pepper

Preheat the oven to 180°CFan/200°C/Gas Mark 6.

Toss the fennel in a bowl with 1 tablespoon of the olive oil, then spread out on an oven tray and roast for 20 minutes until nice and golden and sweet.

Heat the remaining olive oil in a frying pan over a medium heat and fry the sourdough pieces until they are golden, 2–3 minutes. The sourdough needs to be crunchy on the outside but still nice and soft in the middle.

Remove with a slotted spoon, drain on kitchen paper and season with sea salt flakes.

Combine the roasted fennel in a bowl with the tomatoes, sourdough and capers. Add the lemon juice, vinegar and extra virgin olive oil and season with sea salt and fresh cracked pepper. Gently fold in the rocket and basil leaves, then serve.

A staple of Korean kitchens, kimchi is a wonderful introduction to the world of fermented foods. Lactic acid-producing bacteria in fermented foods helps digestion and may also help to boost immunity. Use kimchi as a base for soups and broths or as a side dish. My favourite way to serve it is with eggs, like the Kimchi Omelette with Thai Basil on page 211, but it is also great in a salad, such as the Grapefruit, Kimchi & Cucumber Salad on page 56.

KIMCHI

MAKES 1KG

1 large Chinese cabbage, leaves pulled apart and cut into chunks
2 teaspoons sea salt
½ red onion, sliced
4 spring onions, sliced
3 small carrots, cut into matchsticks
6 radishes, grated

FOR THE PASTE
5 garlic cloves, finely sliced
3cm piece ginger, grated
2 tablespoons caster sugar
2 tablespoons Korean red pepper flakes
3 tablespoons vegetarian fish sauce or light soy sauce
4 tablespoons rice vinegar
1 tablespoon gochujang (Korean fermented red chilli) paste

In a glass or ceramic mixing bowl, combine the cabbage and the salt, mix well and let it sit for an hour. Thoroughly wash the salt off with cold water after an hour and dry the cabbage well.

To make the fermenting paste for the kimchi, mix together the garlic, ginger, sugar, red pepper flakes, vegetarian fish sauce/light soy sauce, vinegar and gochujang paste.

Combine the paste with the cabbage, adding the red onion, spring onions, carrots and radishes. Wash your hands well, then really work it all together (you may want to wear rubber gloves to protect them from the chilli heat).

Transfer the kimchi to a sterile 1.2-litre jar with a sealable lid. Leave the kimchi on a countertop for the first 12 hours and after its initial fermenting stage it can be stored in the fridge.

This kimchi will last for 2 weeks in the fridge, sealed. Use kimchi wherever you can and enjoy its many uses.

Superfood is all around you. You don't have to look for miraculous ingredients on the other side of the world; all you need is seasonal produce close to home. For this recipe I have chosen one of my favourite vegetables: asparagus. It's best in the spring, and in this recipe I maximise the flavour by using the cooking water to create a sauce. The asparagus tips marinated with pomegranate vinegar also enhance the flavour.

ASPARAGUS
WITH FRIED POLENTA & BÉCHAMEL

SERVES 4–6

FOR THE POLENTA
½ teaspoon salt
250g polenta
40g high-quality salted butter

FOR THE ASPARAGUS
1 x 400g bunch green asparagus
8g coarse salt
100g good-quality salted butter
150ml good-quality dry
   white wine
1 garlic clove or 1 teaspoon
   chopped chives
4 mustard leaves (or 1 teaspoon
   Dijon mustard)
sea salt and freshly ground
   black pepper

FOR THE BÉCHAMEL
30g high-quality salted butter
30g plain flour
100g vegetarian grating cheese
sea salt and freshly ground
   black pepper

TO FINISH AND SERVE
fresh mustard flowers
   (if available)
rosemary leaves
2 tablespoons pomegranate
   vinegar

For the polenta, bring 1 litre of water to the boil in a large, heavy-based pan and add the salt. Pour in the polenta in a thin, steady stream, and cook, stirring regularly, until the polenta thickens, about 40 minutes. Pour the polenta into a large, shallow baking tray lined with baking parchment and spread out in an even layer using a spatula. Cool, cover, then chill in the fridge overnight. The next day, cut the polenta into 2 x 5cm rectangles. Heat the butter in a large frying pan over a medium heat, then add the polenta pieces and fry gently, turning, until they are golden brown, about 5 minutes. Set aside.

Clean the asparagus well, trimming away any tough parts of the stem using a sharp knife. Prepare a bowl of iced water. Bring a pan of 900ml water to the boil over a high heat and add the salt. Add the asparagus and cook for 1–2 minutes, or until they have softened but still have some crunch. Use a slotted spoon to transfer the asparagus to the iced water (reserve the cooking water).

Melt the 100g butter in a pan, then add the white wine, garlic or chives and mustard leaves or prepared mustard and season with black pepper. Add the asparagus and cook gently for 4 minutes, until the wine becomes creamy and the asparagus is beginning to brown, keeping the pan moving to roll the asparagus in the butter.

For the béchamel sauce, reduce the half of the asparagus cooking water in a pan to about half its original volume (you should be left with about 200ml). In a separate pan, melt the 30g butter over a low heat, then add the flour and cook, stirring, until the mixture smells toasty, about 2 minutes. Add the reduced 200ml of asparagus water and the grated cheese and whisk well to form a sauce.

When the asparagus is cooked, slice them into long pieces on the diagonal, then transfer to a small bowl. Add mustard flowers (if using), rosemary and the pomegranate vinegar and set aside for 5–6 minutes. The vinegar helps to give acidity to the dish.

To serve, spoon the béchamel sauce onto plates, add a couple of pieces of polenta, and top with the asparagus. Garnish with a few extra mustard flowers and rosemary leaves.

Radishes make perfect finger food and their dazzling colours are sure to bring a smile. High in fibre and vitamin C, they aid digestion and are so lovely and crunchy, with that peppery kick. If you can get hold of radishes with their leaves intact, even better, as you will know they are as fresh as they can be. Radish leaves are wonderful thrown into salads or wilted into soups for an extra hit of pepperiness.

ROASTED RADISHES
WITH BUTTERBEAN HUMMUS, QUINOA & BLACK SESAME

SERVE AS PART OF A MEZZE-STYLE
MEAL

40g red quinoa
20 radishes
1½ tablespoons olive oil
1 portion Butterbean Hummus
(see page 185)
handful flat-leaf parsley,
finely chopped
black sesame seeds, to garnish
extra virgin olive oil, for drizzling
sea salt and freshly ground
black pepper

TO SERVE
lemon wedges
flatbreads, toasted or warmed

Preheat the oven to 180°C Fan/200°C/Gas Mark 6.

Bring a saucepan of salted water to the boil and cook the quinoa over a medium heat for 15–20 minutes until it is tender but still has a little bite. Drain well and leave to cool.

Toss the radishes with the olive oil in a shallow roasting tray, season with salt and pepper and roast in the oven for 5–7 minutes until the radishes have started to turn golden but are still firm and a bit crunchy.

Spread the hummus over the base of a serving platter using a spatula and top with the quinoa followed by the roasted radishes. Sprinkle the parsley over the top along with some black sesame seeds, a drizzle of extra virgin olive oil and a pinch of sea salt flakes.

Serve with toasted or warmed flatbreads to really mop it all up.

These little peppers with smoky salt are addictively delicious on their own but dip them into some velvety smooth hummus and they become healthy snack heaven. If you need to go gluten-free, you could swap the flatbreads for some vegetable crudités.

PADRÓN PEPPERS
WITH BUTTERBEAN HUMMUS & SMOKED SEA SALT

SERVES 3–4 AS PART OF A
MEZZE-STYLE MEAL

**1 portion of Butterbean
  Hummus (see page 185)**
2 tablespoons olive oil
20 padrón peppers
smoked sea salt

TO SERVE
flatbreads, toasted
lemon wedges

Spread the butterbean hummus over the base of a shallow serving bowl or plate using a spatula.

Heat the olive oil in a frying pan over a high heat and sauté the padrón peppers for 5 minutes until they are slightly charred and soft all over.

Using tongs, transfer the charred peppers to a mixing bowl and give them a good season with the smoked sea salt. Arrange the peppers on top of the hummus and serve with toasted flatbreads, lemon wedges and extra smoked salt on the side.

Quinoa is nutrient-dense and provides all nine essential amino acids, making it a very worthwhile salad ingredient. This is a lovely, light, fresh salad and the combination of peas, mint and radishes is deliciously nutritious. Enjoy as a big bowl for lunch or serve as a side dish with the Leek, Cheese & Rocket Spelt-crusted Tart on page 36.

LITTLE GEM, PEA & QUINOA SALAD

SERVES 2 AS A LIGHT MAIN OR
4 AS A SIDE

500ml vegetable stock
**100g red or multi-coloured
quinoa**
150g frozen peas, defrosted
**2 heads little gem lettuce, leaves
separated and cut in half**
2 handfuls rocket
6 radishes, finely sliced
**40g vegetarian pecorino (or
another vegetarian grating
cheese), finely grated**
**8g mint, leaves picked and
roughly torn**
black sesame seeds, to garnish

FOR THE DRESSING
**3 tablespoons extra virgin
olive oil**
1 tablespoon lemon juice
½ tablespoon white wine vinegar
1 teaspoon Dijon mustard
**sea salt and freshly ground
black pepper**

Bring the vegetable stock to the boil in a saucepan, add the quinoa and cook over a medium heat for 15–20 minutes until the quinoa is tender. Drain well and set aside to cool.

Meanwhile, whisk together all the dressing ingredients in a bowl and set aside.

Combine all of the salad ingredients (reserving 20g of the grated cheese) in a large bowl, add the dressing and mix gently.

Serve the salad with the remaining grated cheese scattered over the top, with a sprinkling of black sesame seeds.

A simple raw chopped salad cannot be underestimated. The more vegetables are cooked, the more they lose their nutritional value, so for a mega-boost of healthy goodness opt for raw from time to time. Aside from the nutritional aspect, it is also a wonderful way to taste vegetables. Those living in urban environments may not be able to enjoy pulling a vegetable from the earth and eating it as fresh as it can be, but this is the next best thing.

ASIAN COLESLAW
WITH COCONUT & LEMONGRASS DRESSING

SERVES 4

600g Chinese cabbage,
   shredded
2 carrots, cut into thin
   matchsticks
4 spring onions, sliced into
   rounds
8 radishes, grated
1 small cucumber, cored and
   cut into strips
2 tablespoons cashews, toasted
   and chopped
black sesame seeds, to garnish

FOR THE DRESSING
1 lemongrass stalk, finely
   chopped
1 green chilli, chopped
1 garlic clove, chopped
½ tablespoon grated ginger
10g coriander
15g mint leaves
juice of 2 limes
2 teaspoons caster sugar
1 tablespoon soy sauce
250ml coconut milk
½ teaspoon sea salt

To make the dressing, put all of the ingredients in a blender and blend until smooth. The dressing should be slightly sweet, sour and hot.

For the salad, combine the cabbage, carrots, spring onions, radishes and cucumber in a mixing bowl. Dress with the prepared dressing, mix gently and serve. Top with the chopped cashews and garnish with the sesame seeds.

Beetroot is an excellent source of fibre and vitamin C and gives an earthy richness to dishes. With the healthy fats and protein that nuts and seeds provide, this salad makes for a nutritious lunch.

The rich blue cheese dressing makes slightly more than needed but it is a great dip to serve with crudités of celery and carrot, and it will keep in the fridge for up to 3 days.

BEETROOT & GRAPE SALAD
WITH BLUE CHEESE DRESSING, HAZELNUTS & SESAME SEEDS

SERVES 2 AS A LIGHT MAIN OR
4 AS A SIDE

250g cooked beetroot, diced
    into 2cm pieces
80g red grapes, halved
3 radishes, thinly sliced
100g rocket or spinach
½ tablespoon shelled hazelnuts,
    toasted and chopped
½ tablespoon sesame seeds,
    toasted
2 tablespoons extra virgin
    olive oil
juice of ¼ lemon
crusty bread, to serve

FOR THE BLUE CHEESE DRESSING
25g Stilton (check that it's
    vegetarian), crumbled
60g natural yogurt
60g crème fraîche
1¼ tablespoons cider vinegar
1¼ tablespoons lemon juice
½ tablespoon chives, finely
    chopped
½ tablespoon finely chopped dill
sea salt and freshly ground
    black pepper, to taste

To make the blue cheese dressing, put all the ingredients in a mixing bowl, mix well and season to taste. Set aside.

Combine the rest of the ingredients in a serving bowl and toss gently to combine, then drizzle the blue cheese dressing over the top. Serve as a side dish or as a main for lunch or dinner with some fresh crusty bread.

Is this coleslaw? It's more like a slaw that has lost a little weight and is feeling fighting fit. Traditional mayonnaise-based coleslaw is wonderful but when you fancy that same crunch but want something lighter, try skipping the mayo. Nigella seeds, which are reported to have health benefits such as supporting weight loss to acting as a cold remedy, add a layer of flavour.

BRUSSELS SPROUT SALAD
WITH QUICK-PICKLED CABBAGE, CAPERS & NIGELLA SEEDS

SERVES 4

20 Brussels sprouts, very
   thinly sliced
4 spring onions, finely sliced
1½ tablespoons capers, drained
   and chopped
40g vegetarian grating cheese,
   grated
2 tablespoons nigella seeds
3 tablespoons extra virgin
   olive oil
1 tablespoon lemon juice
handful flat-leaf parsley,
   finely chopped
sea salt and freshly ground
   black pepper

FOR THE QUICK-PICKLED CABBAGE
200ml cider vinegar
2 tablespoons caster sugar
1 tablespoon sea salt
6 peppercorns
6 coriander seeds
400g red cabbage, finely sliced

For the quick-pickled cabbage, bring the vinegar to the boil in a saucepan then add the sugar, salt, peppercorns and coriander seeds. Reduce the heat and simmer for 2–3 minutes.

Put the cabbage in a heatproof glass or ceramic bowl. Pour the hot pickling liquid over the cabbage, then leave to pickle for at least 30 minutes.

Combine the Brussels sprouts, spring onions, capers, cheese and nigella seeds in a separate mixing bowl. Whisk together the oil and lemon juice in a separate small bowl, season with salt and pepper, pour over the sprouts and mix well to combine.

Serve the dressed sprouts topped with the quick-pickled cabbage with the parsley sprinkled on top for a crunchy, crisp and nutritious salad.

This wonderful salad can be enjoyed throughout the year. Try to find carrots with their leafy tops still on, either from a greengrocer or from your local farmers' market. The leaves can be chopped and folded through the salad or used to add to pesto, avoiding any waste. If you are short of the time needed to hang the yogurt for the labneh, you can always just drizzle some yogurt over the salad – but I do recommend taking the time to make it. It's super-handy to have in the fridge and it's lovely spread on flatbread with za'atar, good olive oil and sea salt.

ROAST CARROTS, LENTIL & BULGUR WHEAT SALAD

SERVES 2

100g bulgur wheat
1 tablespoon olive oil
200ml boiling water
300g mixed coloured carrots, washed but not peeled and cut in half horizontally
100g cooked brown lentils from a can or pouch
small handful each coriander and flat-leaf parsley, finely chopped
1 tablespoon extra virgin olive oil
1 tablespoon lemon juice
sea salt and freshly ground black pepper

FOR THE LABNEH
200g full-fat natural or Greek yogurt
pinch of sea salt

FOR THE ZA'ATAR
4 tablespoons dried thyme
4 tablespoons toasted sesame seeds
1 tablespoon dried oregano
4 teaspoons sumac
2 teaspoons marjoram
1 teaspoon sea salt

Begin by making the labneh. It's best to make it the evening before, but it needs to be made at least 4 hours in advance.

Put the yogurt in a piece of muslin or a similar clean cloth, then transfer to a fine sieve. Add the sea salt, then tie the muslin or cloth so it is fairly tight. Place the sieve with the yogurt over a large bowl to catch the liquid as it drains from the yogurt. Set aside to strain for at least 4 hours (or in the fridge overnight). The labneh should be pretty firm in texture when it's ready.

Preheat the oven to 180°C Fan/200°C/Gas Mark 6.

To make the za'atar, put all of the ingredients in a bowl and stir to combine. It will make more than required but the za'atar will last for weeks in a sealed container or jar. Try sprinkling over fried or poached eggs for breakfast or with some bread and quality olive oil.

For the roast carrots and bulgur wheat salad, put the bulgur wheat in a metal mixing bowl, add ½ tablespoon of the olive oil and 1 teaspoon of salt and stir to combine. Pour over the boiling water, wrap the bowl in foil and set aside for 20 minutes.

Meanwhile, put the halved carrots in a baking tray, drizzle with the remaining ½ tablespoon olive oil and season with salt and pepper. Roast for 20–30 minutes, depending on their size. Halfway through roasting, give the carrots a turn. When the carrots are cooked and have a nice colour to them, remove and set aside.

Use a fork to fluff the bulgur wheat a little, then add the lentils, herbs, extra virgin olive oil and lemon juice, stir to combine and season well. Serve the bulgur and lentils on 2 plates or shallow bowls and top with the roasted carrots. Dollop the labneh on top, then sprinkle over 1 tablespoon of the za'atar.

See pages 78–79 for the recipe photograph.

It's pretty easy to love these full-flavoured, meat-like little morsels, and this vegetarian version brings that same joy with every bite. Bulgur wheat is a great healthy ingredient because it is high in fibre and minerals and, being a whole grain, aids in improving digestion. Serve these koftas with a crisp, lemony green-leaf salad to cut through the lovely richness of the tomato sauce.

BUTTERNUT SQUASH & BULGAR WHEAT KOFTAS
WITH TOMATO SAUCE & PINE NUTS

MAKES ABOUT 20

500g butternut squash, peeled
    and chopped into 2cm pieces
200g bulgur wheat
300–400ml boiling water
4 tablespoons olive oil
1 brown onion, finely chopped
2 tablespoons tomato purée
1 egg, beaten
2 tablespoons toasted pine nuts
200g sourdough breadcrumbs
30g vegetarian grating cheese,
    grated, plus extra to serve
2 tablespoons finely chopped
    flat-leaf parsley
sea salt and freshly ground
    black pepper

FOR THE TOMATO SAUCE

2 brown onions, roughly chopped
2 garlic cloves, roughly chopped
1 teaspoon dried oregano
½ teaspoon chilli flakes
2 tablespoons olive oil
1 tablespoon balsamic vinegar
900g tomatoes, halved

Preheat the oven to 180°C Fan/200°C/Gas Mark 6.

For the tomato sauce, put the onions and garlic in a roasting tray along with the oregano and chilli flakes. Season with salt and pepper and drizzle over the olive oil and balsamic vinegar. Put the tomatoes on top, cut-side down, then roast in the oven for 45 minutes. Transfer the slightly cooled contents of the roasting tray to a food processor and blend until fairly smooth.

For the koftas, put the butternut squash in a steamer and steam for 10 minutes or until tender when tested with the tip of a sharp knife. While the butternut is steaming, put the bulgur wheat in a metal mixing bowl and pour over enough of the boiling water to cover. Wrap with foil and set aside for 10–15 minutes until the wheat is tender but still has texture and bite. Drain the butternut, mash and set aside.

Heat 2 tablespoons of the olive oil in a frying pan over a medium heat and cook the onion, stirring, until soft and sweet, for 4–5 minutes. Add the tomato purée and mix to combine. Remove from the heat, then combine the onion and tomato mixture with the steamed butternut and cooked bulgur wheat in a large bowl. Add the egg, 1 tablespoon of pine nuts, breadcrumbs and the cheese. Season and mix well.

Taste the mixture and add salt and pepper as needed, then begin to roll the mixture into about 20 even-sized, oval-shaped pieces. Lay the koftas in a baking tray in a single layer and chill in the fridge for 30–60 minutes to firm up.

Heat the remaining 2 tablespoons of olive oil in a large frying pan over a medium heat and cook the koftas in batches until golden brown. Drain on kitchen paper.

Put the cooked koftas in a roasting tray, ladle over the tomato sauce and bake in the oven for 15–20 minutes until heated through. Serve scattered with the remaining pine nuts, extra grated cheese and the chopped parsley.

See pages 82–83 for the recipe photograph.

Comforting yet fresh, this invigorating broth also happens to be quick to make. Seaweed has thousands of varieties, and coastal cultures around the world have been using it for food for just as many years. Seaweed provides a variety of nourishing minerals, protein and vitamins and, most excitingly of all, it can be sustainably produced. Some forms can grow at an astonishing rate of 15cm a day and it is self-sufficient, taking only what it needs from its surrounding environment, while being resistant to diseases and pests. It needs little in the way of resource-draining interventions such as fertilising, weeding or watering.

MISO, ASPARAGUS & SEAWEED BROTH
WITH UDON NOODLES

SERVES 4

150g dried udon noodles
2 tablespoons sunflower oil
4 shallots, quartered
2cm piece ginger, peeled and
  julienned
2 garlic cloves, finely chopped
1.2 litres vegetable stock
½ tablespoon miso paste
½ tablespoon rice vinegar
1 tablespoon soy sauce, plus
  extra to season
2 tablespoons dried dulse
  (red seaweed)
100g fresh shiitake mushrooms,
  roughly torn
1 bunch asparagus, cut into
  2cm pieces
2 spring onions, finely sliced
sesame seeds, to garnish
Roasted Chilli Oil (see page 90),
  to serve
freshly ground black pepper

Cook the udon noodles according to the packet instructions, drain and set aside.

Heat the sunflower oil in a saucepan over a medium heat and cook the shallots, stirring, for 2–3 minutes until soft. Add the ginger and garlic and cook for 1 further minute.

Pour the vegetable stock into the pan along with the miso, vinegar, soy sauce and dulse. Bring the broth to the boil, add the shiitake mushrooms and reduce the heat to a simmer.

Let the broth simmer away for 20–25 minutes on a low heat. When you are nearly ready to serve, add the asparagus to the broth and cook for 1 minute before removing the broth from the heat. Check to see if the broth needs any extra soy sauce and season with a little pepper.

Put the cooked udon noodles into 4 bowls and ladle over the hot broth. Garnish with the spring onions and a few sesame seeds and serve with the roasted chilli oil on the side.

Butternut squash soup is a very popular vegetarian soup and with good reason. The silky-smooth texture and sweetness of squash always manages to hit the spot. It also lends itself perfectly to the aromas and flavours of South East Asia. The healing properties of turmeric, ginger and lemongrass make this soup sing with goodness and vitality.

BUTTERNUT SQUASH SOUP
WITH TURMERIC, LEMONGRASS & CASHEW SALSA

SERVES 4

2 tablespoons sunflower oil
1 brown onion, roughly chopped
1 carrot, roughly chopped
2 lemongrass stalks, bashed
2 garlic cloves, roughly chopped
1 tablespoon grated ginger
20g turmeric (fresh), finely
    chopped
1 red chilli, roughly chopped
1 tablespoon chopped coriander
    stalks
2 tablespoons soy sauce
1 tablespoon caster sugar
1.2kg butternut squash, peeled
    and cut into 2–3cm chunks
900ml water
400ml can coconut milk
juice of 1 lime

FOR THE CASHEW SALSA
60g toasted cashews, chopped
4 spring onions, finely chopped
2 tablespoons chopped coriander
½ red chilli, deseeded and
    finely chopped
juice of ½ lime
1 teaspoon soy sauce

FOR THE FRIED RICE NOODLES
sunflower oil, for shallow frying
60g vermicelli rice noodles

Heat the 2 tablespoons of sunflower oil in a large saucepan and add the onion and carrot. Cook on a low heat for 5–10 minutes until soft and sweet. Add the lemongrass, garlic, ginger, turmeric, chilli and coriander stalks, then cook for a further 2–3 minutes.

Add the soy sauce and caster sugar and cook until the sugar has dissolved. Add the butternut squash to the pan with the water and bring to the boil. Reduce to a simmer and cook for 30–40 minutes.

While the soup is simmering away, mix all of the ingredients for the cashew salsa in a bowl and set aside.

For the fried rice noodles, heat 3–4 tablespoons of sunflower oil in a frying pan and shallow-fry the noodles for 2 minutes. You will know when they are ready – they will puff up and turn white in colour. Drain on kitchen paper and set aside.

At the end of the soup's cooking time, add the coconut milk and lime juice. Remove the lemongrass stalks and discard. Transfer the soup to a blender and blend until smooth.

Serve the soup in bowls topped with the cashew salsa and some fried rice noodles to finish.

MasterChef Tip: *Anytime you have coriander stalks left after picking the leaves, save them to use in curry pastes, stir fries and soups. When cooked they are wonderfully aromatic and really help enhance the flavour of certain dishes, plus the whole herb is being used, leaving you with precious little waste.*

GABRIEL JONSSON MASTERCHEF SWEDEN CHAMPION 2019

For me, cooking is about taking advantage of what nature gives us and respecting it fully. I grew up on a farm, so I've always had a huge respect for all living animals and plants. I always think that food tastes better if the ingredients come from suppliers and places you know, or are local to you. This beautiful salad makes the most of the produce available to us locally, and is incredibly healthy too. I hope you enjoy this recipe.

BEETROOT & WHEATBERRY SALAD
WITH WARM VINAIGRETTE

SERVES 4

100g wheatberries (commonly known as wheat grain in the UK), or spelt grain
4 beetroot, with leaves
1½ tablespoons rapeseed oil
1 tablespoon red wine vinegar
1 teaspoon runny honey
sea salt and freshly ground black pepper

TO SERVE
40g walnuts, chopped
sage leaves
thyme leaves

Cook the wheatberries according to the packet instructions, but for 2 minutes less than the recommended time, then drain.

Cut off the leaves and stems from the beetroot and cut these into 1cm size pieces, then set aside. Wash the beetroot well and cut them thinly, ideally using a mandoline.

Heat the oil in a frying pan and, when hot, add the drained wheatberries and cook, stirring, for a few minutes until they take on some colour. Add the beetroot tops and stems and cook for a further 30 seconds. Add the vinegar and honey, stir well and season with salt and pepper.

Arrange the beetroot slices over the base of each plate. Spoon over the wheatberries, beetroot stems and leaves and the warm vinaigrette. Top with chopped walnuts and herbs, and enjoy.

These noodles are wonderfully fresh and quick. Soba noodles made from 100 per cent buckwheat flour have higher levels of fibre and protein and fewer calories compared to noodles or pasta made from refined wheat. The roasted chilli oil gives the noodles a real kick while the cucumber provides a nice soothing balance.

SOBA NOODLES
WITH GINGER, CUCUMBER & ROASTED CHILLI OIL

SERVES 4

400g dried soba noodles
2 tablespoons sunflower oil
6 spring onions, thinly sliced, white and green parts separated
25g ginger, peeled and cut into thin strips
2 garlic cloves, finely chopped
100ml soy sauce
2 teaspoons toasted sesame oil
50ml mirin

FOR THE ROASTED CHILLI OIL
3 tablespoons sunflower oil, plus extra (optional)
6 garlic cloves, finely chopped
2 shallots, finely chopped
4 tablespoons chilli flakes
2 tablespoons soy sauce
1 teaspoon sea salt

TO SERVE
2 cucumbers, cored and peeled into ribbons
sesame seeds, to garnish

Begin by making the roasted chilli oil. Heat the oil in a saucepan over a medium heat and fry the garlic and shallots for 1–2 minutes. Add the chilli flakes and cook for another 3–4 minutes on a low heat. If it is looking a little dry, add a bit more oil. Add the soy sauce and salt then set aside and leave to cool. This recipe makes more chilli oil than needed but it will keep for up to 2 weeks in a sealed jar in the fridge.

For the noodles, cook the soba noodles following the instructions on the packet, drain and leave to cool.

Heat the oil in a wok over a medium to high heat and fry the white parts of the spring onions along with the ginger and garlic for 1 minute. Add the soy sauce, sesame oil and mirin followed by the cooked soba noodles. Toss to combine and check that the noodles are heated through.

Serve the noodles with the cucumber ribbons on top, then scatter over the sesame seeds and the reserved spring onion greens, with some roasted chilli oil on the side.

MasterChef Tip: *You can use a teaspoon or a dessertspoon to peel the ginger. You will have much less wastage compared to using a peeler or a knife as it will contour more easily into the ginger.*

Spelt, an ancient grain, was one of the first used to make bread. It has a wonderful nutty flavour and provides higher levels of dietary fibre than wheat. This is a lovely, fresh and vibrant dish to make in spring, when young vegetables really start to come into their own.

SPRING GARDEN SPELT RISOTTO

SERVES 4

2 tablespoons olive oil
4 shallots, finely chopped
2 garlic cloves, finely chopped
150ml white wine
200g pearled spelt
25g unsalted butter
1 litre vegetable stock, hot
1 bunch asparagus, stems cut into
   1cm pieces, tips whole
150g frozen peas, defrosted
100g baby spinach
40g vegetarian grating cheese,
   grated, plus extra for serving
small handful flat-leaf parsley,
   finely chopped
sea salt and freshly ground
   black pepper

Heat the olive oil in a wide, heavy-based saucepan over a medium heat. Add the shallots and cook for 2–3 minutes, stirring regularly (don't let the shallots take on any colour). Add the garlic and cook for another minute.

Add the white wine to the pan and cook for 1 minute before adding the spelt and butter. Melt the butter to coat the spelt well, then add 250ml of the hot vegetable stock. As the risotto starts to absorb the stock, add a little more and repeat the process, cooking over a medium heat for 20–25 minutes, stirring regularly.

When the spelt is tender, add the asparagus, peas and spinach and heat them through. Stir in the cheese and season with a little salt and a good amount of cracked black pepper. If the risotto looks a little dry, add a bit more stock or some water.

Serve with the chopped parsley and a little extra freshly grated cheese on top.

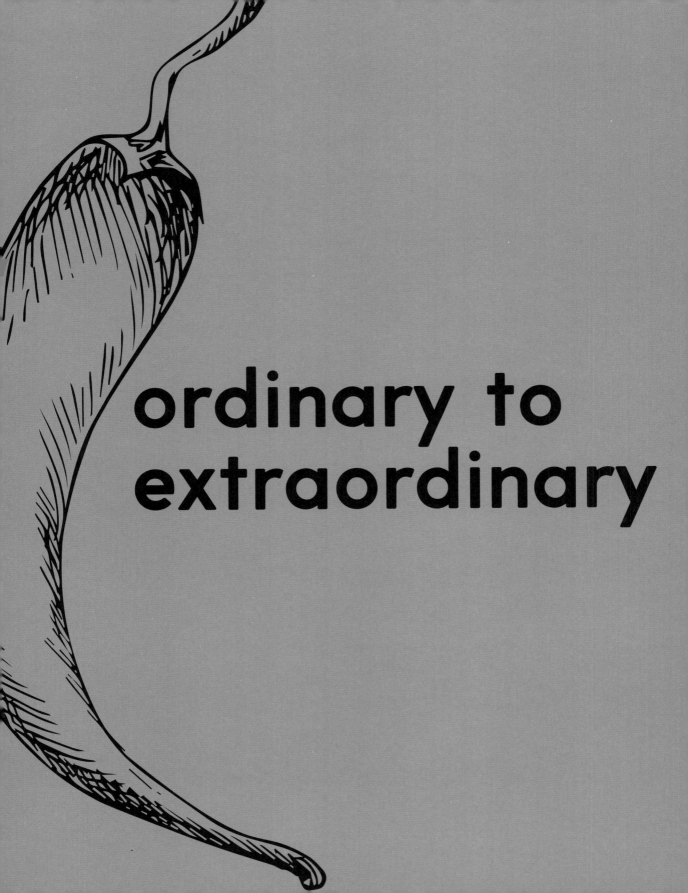

ordinary to
extraordinary

What's wonderful about many warm-climate food cultures is that a meal doesn't have to consist of just one or two dishes, but could be a selection of smaller dishes served mezze-style. This vegetarian makeover of sesame prawn toasts has the quintessential springy texture but uses mushrooms in place of prawns. It's just made for sharing.

MUSHROOM TOASTS
WITH BLACK VINEGAR DIP

MAKES 16

250g mushrooms (mix of
    shiitake and chestnut),
    roughly chopped
2 spring onions, chopped
1 tablespoon chopped
    coriander stems
1 egg white
2 teaspoons caster sugar
1 teaspoon sea salt
½ teaspoon toasted sesame oil
sunflower or vegetable oil,
    for deep frying
4 large slices sourdough,
    each quartered
sesame seeds, for sprinkling

FOR THE BLACK VINEGAR DIP
4 tablespoons Chinese
    black vinegar
2 tablespoons soy sauce
½ teaspoon toasted sesame oil
1 shallot, finely chopped
2 teaspoons caster sugar
½ teaspoon sea salt
½ tablespoon grated ginger
½ teaspoon chilli flakes

Put the mushrooms, spring onions, coriander stems, egg white, caster sugar, salt and sesame oil in a food processor and whizz to a rough paste. Cover and chill the mushroom mixture in the fridge for 30–40 minutes.

Meanwhile, for the black vinegar dip, combine all of the ingredients in a bowl, stir to combine and set aside.

If you have a deep-fat fryer, put the sunflower or vegetable oil in it and set the temperature to 180°C. Otherwise, fill a large, heavy-based saucepan one-third full with the oil. Heat until the oil reaches 180°C when tested on a food thermometer. The oil is hot enough when a small piece of bread dropped into it floats to the top and turns golden in 20 seconds.

Spoon the mushroom mixture evenly over the sourdough pieces, then liberally sprinkle the top of the toasts with sesame seeds.

Carefully lower the mushroom toasts into the hot oil using a slotted spoon and fry for 4–5 minutes (you may need to cook them in batches depending on the size of your fryer/pan). Turn the toasts over halfway. Remove the toasts using the slotted spoon and drain on kitchen paper. Serve with the black vinegar dip.

Beans on toast. You quickly open a can, heat and, hey presto! Breakfast is served. Why does it feel so naughty? Shop-bought baked beans have their place, but once you've made your own the good old canned variety will never quite seem the same. If you're a fan of smoky flavours, I would recommend getting your hands on some quality liquid smoke (a little goes a long way). Shiitake or oyster mushrooms provide a texture similar to pulled pork, making this close to the kind of thing you might get at your favourite weekend brunch café.

SMOKY BAKED BEANS
WITH WILD MUSHROOMS

SERVES 4–5

250g haricot beans, soaked overnight
2 tablespoons olive oil
1 red onion, chopped
2 garlic cloves, finely chopped
150g mixed wild mushrooms (shiitake, oyster), roughly chopped
1 teaspoon thyme leaves
1 teaspoon smoked paprika
½ teaspoon chilli flakes
50ml cider vinegar
400ml vegetable stock
400g can chopped tomatoes
1 tablespoon tomato purée
½ tablespoon liquid smoke
1½ tablespoons soft dark brown sugar
½ tablespoon maple syrup
sea salt and freshly ground black pepper

Drain the haricot beans, rinse under fresh cold water, put in a saucepan and add water to cover. Bring the beans to the boil then reduce the heat to medium and cook the beans for 30–40 minutes until soft but still with a little bite and texture. Drain, let cool and set aside.

Heat the olive oil in a heavy-based saucepan over a medium heat and cook the onion, garlic and mushrooms, stirring, for 3–4 minutes. Add the thyme, smoked paprika and chilli flakes and cook for another minute.

Add the vinegar, vegetable stock, chopped tomatoes and tomato purée. Add the cooked haricot beans and bring to the boil. Reduce the heat to a simmer then add the liquid smoke, sugar and maple syrup. Cook the beans for 50 minutes to 1 hour, covered.

The beans should be a lovely rich red in colour and have a balanced sweetness to them. Taste the beans and add a little salt and cracked pepper as needed before serving.

Serve on grilled sourdough, or with Courgette, Smoked Cheddar & Jalapeño Bread (see page 14) for a delicious start to the day.

The mighty Scotch egg is a much-loved pub snack. Biting into a perfectly golden fried sphere is a moment to savour. Chickpeas are a delightful swap for the meaty layer, being high in protein and calling to mind another famous fried morsel, the falafel. Dipped into gut-healthy kimchi mayo, this is a classic with a gorgeous tangy twist.

CHICKPEA SCOTCH EGGS
WITH KIMCHI MAYO

MAKES 4

5 eggs
sunflower oil, for deep frying
   and frying
1 medium onion, finely chopped
1 garlic clove, finely chopped
½ red chilli, chopped
400g can chickpeas, drained
small handful coriander, chopped
zest of 1 lime and juice of ½
3 tablespoons plain flour
80g breadcrumbs
sea salt and freshly ground
   black pepper

FOR THE KIMCHI MAYO
80g Kimchi (see page 63)
80g mayonnaise

For the kimchi mayo, put the kimchi and the mayonnaise in a blender and blend until smooth. Transfer to a small bowl and set aside in the fridge until needed.

Bring a saucepan of water to the boil and use a spoon to gently lower in 4 of the eggs. Gently boil for 6½ minutes, then remove from the water and plunge the eggs into cold water to prevent further cooking. When the eggs are cool enough to handle, peel them carefully and chill in the fridge.

Heat 1 tablespoon of the sunflower oil in a saucepan over a medium heat, add the onion, garlic and chilli and cook, stirring, for 5 minutes until they are soft.

Transfer the mix to a food processor along with the chickpeas and coriander and whizz to a rough paste. Combine the chickpea paste in a mixing bowl with the lime zest and juice, then season well with salt and pepper. Chill the mixture in the fridge for at least 30 minutes to firm up.

Put the flour, breadcrumbs and the remaining egg (whisked) in 3 separate shallow bowls. Take the chickpea mixture from the fridge along with the soft-boiled eggs.

Divide the chickpea mix into 4 even quantities. Flatten them on a clean work surface and place 1 egg in the centre of each portion. Use your hands to carefully mould the mixture around each egg, to fully enclose.

Once the eggs are enclosed in the chickpea mixture, roll one at a time in the flour first, followed by the beaten egg and finally the breadcrumbs to coat them evenly. Place the 4 crumbed eggs on a plate and chill in the fridge for a further 30 minutes to firm up again.

While the scotch eggs are chilling, if you have a deep-fat fryer, put the sunflower oil in it and set the temperature to 180°C. Otherwise, fill a large, heavy-based saucepan one-third full with the oil. Heat until the oil reaches 180°C when tested on a food thermometer. The oil is hot enough when a small piece of bread dropped into it floats to the top and turns golden in 20 seconds.

Carefully lower the scotch eggs into the oil using a spoon and cook for 2–3 minutes until they are nice and golden brown. If necessary, cook in batches. Remove using a slotted spoon and drain on kitchen paper. Let rest for 5 minutes then serve with the kimchi mayo.

What's not to love about cheesy croquettes? That moment of anticipation when you bite into a warm, crispy, crumbed croquette and that lovely melted cheese. Croquettes also provide an opportunity to add an element of surprise, which makes them that little bit more special. This recipe uses a few fresh basil leaves to complement the creamy goat's cheese.

GOAT'S CHEESE & BASIL CROQUETTES
WITH HONEY & VINEGAR DIP

MAKES 8

40g plain flour
1 egg, beaten
100g panko breadcrumbs
320g soft goat's cheese
16 basil leaves
**sunflower or vegetable oil for
    deep frying**
**sea salt and freshly ground
    black pepper**

FOR THE DRESSING
4 tablespoons runny honey
**2 tablespoons aged balsamic
    vinegar**
**sea salt and freshly ground
    black pepper**

Lay out 3 separate shallow bowls on a work surface and fill each one with the flour, the egg and the panko breadcrumbs. Season each with a little salt and cracked black pepper.

Divide the goat's cheese into 8 equal-sized balls. Take 1 ball at a time and, using your finger, make an indentation into each. Place 2 basil leaves into each indentation and roll each ball back over itself to enclose the basil.

Roll the goat's cheese balls in the flour first, then dip into the beaten egg, then finally roll in the breadcrumbs. Put the croquettes on a plate and chill in the fridge for 30–40 minutes to firm up.

Meanwhile, for the dressing, mix the honey and balsamic vinegar in a small bowl, season well with freshly cracked black pepper and set aside.

If you have a deep-fat fryer, put the sunflower or vegetable oil in it and set the temperature to 180°C. Otherwise, fill a large, heavy-based saucepan one-third full with the oil. Heat until the oil reaches 180°C when tested on a food thermometer. The oil is hot enough when a small piece of bread dropped into it floats to the top and turns golden in 20 seconds.

When the oil is hot, deep fry the balls in 2 batches for 2–3 minutes until golden and floating on the surface of the oil. Remove using a slotted spoon, then drain on kitchen paper.

Serve the croquettes with the honey and vinegar dip for a perfect little pre-dinner party nibble.

MasterChef Tip: *Try to leave the croquettes to rest and cool slightly before eating. It may be hard but it will be worthwhile, as you will get the full flavour of the cheese.*

Grilled or barbecued corn on the cob slathered in butter screams sun and summer. The wonderful sweetness and pop-in-your-mouth texture are one of life's simple pleasures. Simple is great but there's often a way to make things just that little bit better. Add some zingy lime, fiery jalapeño and salty grated cheese, and have yourself a seriously good side dish for al fresco evenings.

CORN ON THE COB
WITH LIME & JALAPEÑO BUTTER & CHEESE

SERVES 4 AS A SIDE

75g unsalted butter, softened
1 garlic clove, finely chopped
2 tablespoons chopped pickled jalapeños
zest of 2 limes
1 teaspoon sea salt
4 cobs of corn
20g vegetarian grating cheese, finely grated
olive oil, for drizzling
chopped coriander, to garnish

Mix together the butter, garlic, jalapeños, lime zest and salt in a bowl. Set aside.

Bring a large pan of water to the boil, add the corn cobs and cook for 5–7 minutes, until the kernels are tender and cooked through. Drain well and pat dry.

Heat a frying pan over a high heat. When hot, add the corn to the pan with a drizzle of olive oil and regularly move the corn around the pan, letting the corn slightly char in places, for about 5 minutes.

When the cobs are nice and charred, turn the heat down and add the lime and jalapeño butter to the pan. Baste the corn cobs with the butter but don't let the butter burn.

Serve the corn cobs on a serving platter with the melted butter from the pan spooned over and the grated cheese sprinkled on top. Garnish with chopped coriander.

Try serving these as a barbecue-style side with Celeriac Steaks with Chimichurri & Apple Chilli Coleslaw (see page 151).

Corn fritters and brunch go hand-in-hand. Packed with vibrancy and flavour, a batch of these are a great way to ease into the weekend. Mashed avocado is the classic accompaniment but, depending on where you live, those avocados may have come from a long way away. Mashed peas are a great substitute and they provide added freshness, while helping to keep ingredients a little closer to home.

CORN FRITTERS
WITH SMASHED PEAS, QUICK-PICKLED ONIONS & POACHED EGGS

SERVES 6

80ml sunflower oil
1 batch Corn Fritter batter
   (see page 118)

FOR THE QUICK-PICKLED ONIONS
100ml cider vinegar
1 tablespoon caster sugar
1 teaspoon sea salt
3 black peppercorns
3 coriander seeds
½ red onion, sliced

FOR THE SMASHED PEAS
250g frozen peas, defrosted
handful mint leaves, roughly
   chopped
1 tablespoon extra virgin olive oil
½ tablespoon lemon juice
sea salt and freshly ground
   black pepper

FOR THE POACHED EGGS
1 tablespoon white vinegar
6 eggs

TO SERVE
100g crème fraîche
50g watercress or rocket

Preheat the oven to 100°C Fan/120°C/Gas Mark ½.

The day or night before, make the quick-pickled onions to allow enough time for the flavour to develop. You can always make a larger quantity of the onions to use in sandwiches or with cheese.

Bring the vinegar to the boil in a saucepan and add the sugar, salt, peppercorns and coriander seeds. Leave to simmer for a few minutes, then remove from the heat and add the sliced onion. Leave to cool, then transfer to a sterilised jar.

For the smashed peas, put the peas, mint, olive oil and lemon juice in a food processor or blender and whizz, leaving it with some texture (don't over-blend it and let it turn into a purée). Season with salt and pepper and set aside.

To make the fritters, heat the sunflower oil in a frying pan over a medium to high heat. When hot, drop heaped dessertspoons of the corn fritter batter into the pan. Cook the fritters for 2–3 minutes on each side, turning carefully using a fish slice. Drain on kitchen paper while you cook the remaining fritters. Once all of the fritters are cooked, put them on an oven tray and keep warm in the oven while you poach the eggs.

Bring a large saucepan of water to the boil and add a tablespoon of white vinegar to the pan. Once boiling, turn the heat down to a simmer and use a slotted spoon to stir the water in a circular motion to create a vortex before cracking the eggs into the water one by one. Poach the eggs for 3 minutes 30–45 seconds then carefully remove the eggs with a slotted spoon and put on a clean tea towel.

To serve, put the smashed peas onto the plates first, followed by the corn fritters, some crème fraîche and then the pickled onions, watercress or rocket and add a poached egg on the side.

See pages 106–107 for the recipe photograph.

The utter joy of biting into crisp golden puff pastry followed by the warm comfort of minced ... vegetables? Yes, vegetables. Mushrooms, with their wonderful earthy flavour and texture, makes these 'sausage' rolls suitable for everyone. You can serve these with a range of condiments, but I recommend taking the time to make a red pepper chilli jam. Its sweet spiciness complements the savoury earthiness of the mushrooms and lentils so well.

LENTIL & MUSHROOM 'SAUSAGE' ROLLS

MAKES 10

200g chestnut mushrooms, roughly chopped
3 shallots, roughly chopped
1 garlic clove, roughly chopped
1 tablespoon thyme leaves
1 tablespoon olive oil
200g cooked and cooled brown lentils
60g panko breadcrumbs
20g mature Cheddar, grated
½ tablespoon Dijon mustard
1 x 320g puff pastry sheet
plain flour, for dusting
1 egg, beaten
sesame seeds
Red Pepper Chilli Jam (page 193) to serve
sea salt and freshly ground black pepper

Whizz the mushrooms, shallots, garlic and thyme in a food processor until the mixture has the texture of breadcrumbs.

Heat the olive oil in a frying pan over a medium heat, add the mushroom and shallot mixture and cook for 10 minutes or until soft.

Combine the lentils, breadcrumbs, Cheddar and Dijon mustard in a mixing bowl. Add the cooked mushroom and shallot mixture and stir to combine well. Season with salt and black pepper then chill in the fridge for 15–20 minutes.

Lay the puff pastry sheet on a lightly floured work surface and cut in half horizontally. Spread half of the lentil and mushroom mixture horizontally along each piece of pastry. Roll the pastry over the filling to form 2 tight logs. Transfer the logs to a baking tray lined with baking parchment and chill them in the fridge for 20 minutes.

Preheat the oven to 180°C Fan/200°C/Gas Mark 6.

Remove the logs from the fridge and use a pastry brush to brush each log with the beaten egg, then cut each log into 5 equal pieces. Sprinkle sesame seeds over the top of them along with a sprinkle of sea salt and cracked pepper. Bake in the oven for 15–20 minutes until the pastry is golden and crisp.

Let the rolls rest for 5–10 minutes before serving. Serve with red pepper jam or tomato ketchup on the side and sit back and look at your family and friends' expressions of 'What, these aren't meat?'

MasterChef Tip: *The sausage rolls freeze amazingly well. You can make a large batch and, once chilled, cut them as required and freeze. Defrost as you need them, egg wash and sprinkle with sesame seeds, and bake as above.*

See pages 110–111 for the recipe photograph.

Jackfruit is such a versatile fruit and a relatively new 'greatest hit' in the vegetarian world. Given the right treatment, its flesh can be unbelievably similar to that of pulled pork or shredded chicken. Add the lovely smoky chipotle braise and liquid smoke, and these tacos will guarantee that any new veggie convert won't be missing meat at all.

PULLED JACKFRUIT TACOS
WITH CHIPOTLE, CHARRED CORN & COLESLAW

MAKES 10

2 tablespoons sunflower oil
1 brown onion, finely chopped
2 garlic cloves, finely chopped
1 large chipotle chilli in Adobo
    sauce, chopped
1 teaspoon ground cumin
1 teaspoon ground coriander
1 teaspoon dried oregano
1 teaspoon smoked paprika
120g tomato ketchup
250ml water
½ tablespoon liquid smoke
2 x 400g cans young jackfruit in
    water, drained and shredded
sea salt and freshly ground
    black pepper

FOR THE CHARRED CORN
2 cobs of corn, kernels removed

FOR THE COLESLAW
150g red cabbage, finely
    shredded
1 medium carrot, cut into
    thin matchsticks
4 spring onions, finely sliced
juice of ½ lime
80g soured cream, plus extra
    to serve
small handful coriander, chopped

TO SERVE
10 corn or wheat tortillas
avocado slices
lime wedges
hot sauce

Heat the oil in a saucepan over a medium heat, add the onion and garlic and cook, stirring, for 1–2 minutes until they have softened. Add the chipotle chilli, cumin, coriander, oregano and smoked paprika and cook for a further minute. Add the ketchup, water and liquid smoke and bring to the boil. Reduce the heat to low and add the jackfruit. Simmer for 15–20 minutes, until thickened, then season well with sea salt.

While the jackfruit is cooking, char the corn kernels in a dry frying pan over a high heat for 2–3 minutes until they start to get some dark charred marks. Add a few tablespoons of water to the pan to allow the corn to steam and cook through for a further 1–2 minutes then set aside.

For the coleslaw, mix all of the ingredients together in a bowl and season with salt and pepper.

In a separate frying pan, toast the tortillas over a medium heat until they are warm and lightly toasted but not crisp.

To make the tacos, start by putting some coleslaw in the centre of each tortilla, then top with pulled jackfruit followed by the charred corn kernels. Serve with extra soured cream, slices of avocado, lime wedges and hot sauce for the ones who like it hot.

This dish is very close to my heart because it reminds me of how my mother would fool me into eating jackfruit by calling it a meat curry. It's a home-style curry, and recreating it for *MasterChef* was challenging because I had to turn it into gourmet food. You can easily double this and use a 20cm tart case.

KATHAL KI DASTAN
THE STORY OF THE JACKFRUIT

SERVES 2–3 AS A SNACK

FOR THE TART CASE

100g plain flour
30g chilled salted butter, cubed
15g fresh oregano, finely
   chopped, plus extra to garnish
1 teaspoon garam masala
½ teaspoon ground turmeric
salt, to taste

FOR THE JACKFRUIT CURRY

1.5cm piece ginger
8–10 garlic cloves
2 tablespoons mustard oil,
   or vegetable oil
1 onion, chopped
1 green chilli, chopped
1 small tomato, chopped
250g jackfruit (fresh or canned),
   chopped
½ teaspoon turmeric powder
½ teaspoon chilli powder
1 teaspoon cumin powder
½ teaspoon garam masala
15g coriander, chopped

FOR THE JACKFRUIT MOUSSE

80g jackfruit (fresh or canned),
   peeled and diced
25g single cream
30ml milk
pinch of freshly grated nutmeg
1–1½ teaspoons black pepper

Preheat the oven to 160°C Fan/180°C/Gas Mark 4. For the tart case, combine all the ingredients in a mixing bowl. Using your fingertips, mix the butter into the flour, spices and herbs until the mixture resembles breadcrumbs. Add just enough chilled water, one teaspoon at a time, to bring the mixture together as a dough.

Use your hands to form the dough into a ball (do not knead excessively) then put it in a 15cm tart case with a removable base and, using your fingertips, press it into the tin to evenly cover the base and sides. Use a fork to prick the base of the tart base all over so it doesn't puff up in the oven. You could chill the pastry in the fridge for 20 minutes before baking to set it well, otherwise you can bake straightaway. Bake for 10–12 minutes until it has a golden brown colour, then remove and set aside to cool.

For the jackfruit curry, crush the ginger and garlic to a paste. Heat the oil in a large lidded saucepan over a medium heat then add the onion and cook, stirring, until it turns golden brown, 3–4 minutes. Add the ginger and garlic paste and the chopped green chilli and cook, stirring, for 4–5 minutes. Add 2 tablespoons of water, cook for another 2 minutes, then taste and add salt as needed. Add the tomato and cook, stirring, for another 5–7 minutes, until the oil separates out. Add the jackfruit, mix it well then add all the dried spices and mix to combine. Cover the pan with a lid, turn down the heat to low and simmer for 10 minutes.

After 10 minutes, check the consistency, adding a little water if needed, and cook with the lid off for 2–3 minutes. At the end of the cooking time, add the chopped coriander leaves.

For the jackfruit mousse, if using fresh jackfruit, place the diced jackfruit in a pressure cooker with double the amount of water and cook for 4 whistles, or simmer the jackfruit and 4 times the amount of water in a saucepan over a low heat until the jackfruit starts to fall apart when pressed, around 12–15 minutes. Drain and then blend the jackfruit and all the ingredients in a blender to make a smooth paste. If it's a little runny, chill in the fridge for 10 minutes.

Transfer to a piping bag fitted with a nozzle of your choice. Fill the tart case with the jackfruit curry, then pipe the jackfruit mousse on top. Serve garnished with a few fresh oregano leaves.

I can remember the first time I ate a hash brown as a child and my initial reaction was WOW. It was a time long before I knew how to cook, and those hash browns would have been straight out of a packet from a freezer. But how I loved them. With so much convenience food at our disposal it's easy to take the ready-prepared option, but with skills and know-how, you can easily make your own. Having a mix of potato and another root vegetable along with some fragrant herbs elevates these from simple to remarkable.

CELERIAC & SAGE HASH BROWNS
WITH SPICED APPLE CHUTNEY

MAKES 12

200g celeriac, grated
400g Maris Piper potatoes, grated
1 brown onion, grated
12 sage leaves, finely chopped
small handful flat-leaf parsley, finely chopped
1 egg, beaten
2 tablespoons plain flour
80ml olive oil
2 handfuls watercress
fried eggs, to serve (optional)
sea salt and freshly ground black pepper

FOR THE SPICED APPLE CHUTNEY
1 tablespoon sunflower oil
2 shallots, finely chopped
10g ginger, grated
½ teaspoon curry powder
½ teaspoon ground cinnamon
½ teaspoon black mustard seeds
½ teaspoon chilli flakes
4 Granny Smith apples, cored and chopped
40g caster sugar
40ml water

Preheat the oven to 180°C Fan/200°C/Gas Mark 6.

Begin by making the spiced apple chutney. Heat the oil in a saucepan over a medium heat, add the shallots and ginger and cook, stirring, for 1–2 minutes. Add the curry powder, cinnamon, mustard seeds and chilli flakes, then cook for 30 seconds to release their aromas. Add the apples, sugar and water then bring to the boil. Reduce the heat and simmer for 15–20 minutes, until the apples have broken down and the chutney has thickened.

For the hash browns, put the grated celeriac and potato in a clean tea towel, then put the tea towel into a sieve add a couple of pinches of salt to help draw out the water. Squeeze the celeriac and potato very well to try to get as much moisture out of them as you can.

Combine the celeriac, potato, onion, sage, parsley, egg and flour in a mixing bowl. Mix well and season with salt and pepper.

Heat the olive oil in a frying pan over a medium to high heat. When the oil is hot, drop heaped dessertspoons of the hash brown batter into the hot oil, flattening them gently using a spatula. Cook each hash brown for 2–3 minutes until they are crispy and golden, working in batches. Drain the cooked hash browns on kitchen paper and, when all the hash browns are cooked, transfer to the oven for 10 minutes.

Serve the hash browns with the chutney and the watercress. If you like, add some fried eggs for a more substantial weekend brunch.

A lightly toasted, fluffy bun presents endless possibilities. You can keep it simple or really raise the flavour game, as with these burgers. Gochujang, a fermented chilli paste, is wonderfully savoury, sweet and spicy. Combine it with crispy corn and coriander fritters and a mango salsa and you have a taste explosion. You can use canned corn but for a superior fritter, use fresh corn from the cob.

CORN FRITTER BURGERS
WITH MANGO SALSA & GOCHUJANG MAYO

SERVES 4

250g corn kernels (from about 3 cobs)
½ red pepper, finely chopped
½ red onion, finely chopped
12g coriander, chopped
zest of 1 lime
50g polenta
110g plain flour
2 teaspoons baking powder
1 teaspoon smoked paprika
170ml buttermilk
2 eggs, beaten
30g unsalted butter, melted
sunflower or vegetable oil for deep frying
sea salt

FOR THE GOCHUJANG MAYO
3 tablespoons mayonnaise
1½ tablespoons gochujang (Korean fermented chilli) paste

FOR THE MANGO SALSA
½ mango, peeled and diced
1 tablespoon red onion, diced
1 tablespoon tomato, deseeded and diced
½ tablespoon lime juice
6g coriander, chopped

TO SERVE
4 brioche burger buns
8 baby gem leaves, washed
12 cucumber slices

For the gochujang mayo, combine the mayonnaise and the gochujang in a bowl and set aside.

For the mango salsa, combine all of the salsa ingredients in a bowl, season with a little salt and set aside.

To make the corn fritters, place 3 large bowls on a work surface. In one bowl combine the corn kernels, pepper, onion, coriander and lime zest. In the next bowl mix together the polenta, flour, baking powder, smoked paprika and 1 teaspoon of salt. In the last bowl mix together the buttermilk, eggs and melted butter.

Begin by folding together the corn and pepper mixture with the polenta and flour mixture. Mix well, then add the contents to the bowl with the buttermilk, eggs and butter, so it's all in one bowl. Gently fold the mixture together, trying not to overwork the mixture. Chill in the fridge for 30–60 minutes to allow the batter to firm up.

If you have a deep-fat fryer, put the sunflower or vegetable oil in it and set the temperature to 180°C. Otherwise, fill a large, heavy-based saucepan one-third full with the oil. Heat until the oil reaches 180°C when tested on a food thermometer. The oil is hot enough when a small piece of bread dropped into it floats to the top and turns golden in 20 seconds.

Working in batches if needed, carefully drop 8 heaped dessertspoons of the fritter batter into the hot oil and fry for 4–5 minutes, carefully moving the fritters around the fryer/pan. Remove using a slotted spoon and drain on kitchen paper. Let rest while you toast the brioche buns.

Spread a little of the gochujang mayo on each side of the toasted buns. Place 2 gem lettuce leaves on each bun followed by 2 fritters, 3 cucumber slices and some mango salsa. Serve with the Sweet Potato Fries with Sriracha & Lime Yogurt (see page 189).

Since the potato arrived in Europe from South America in the seventeenth century it has become one of our favourite vegetables, one we eat in so many different ways. Potato hash is an any-time-of-day dish, and a good one will have wonderful bits that are crisp and golden on the outside and soft and fluffy in the middle. Pair this with spices and fresh yogurt and you're in potato heaven.

CURRIED POTATO HASH
WITH ROAST PEPPER, LENTILS & YOGURT

SERVES 2

1 red pepper
2½ tablespoons olive oil
400g new potatoes
80g brown lentils
½ red onion, roughly sliced
25g butter
1 garlic clove, finely chopped
½ tablespoon curry powder
½ teaspoon ground cumin
½ teaspoon ground coriander
½ teaspoon chilli flakes
½ teaspoon ground turmeric
100g baby spinach
sea salt, to season

TO SERVE
125g natural yogurt
small handful mint leaves,
   finely sliced

Preheat the oven to 180°C Fan/200°C/Gas Mark 6. Put the red pepper on a roasting tray and drizzle ½ tablespoon of olive oil over it. Roast for 15–20 minutes until soft. When the pepper is cool enough to handle, peel off the skin (discard) and scrape away the seeds. Cut the roasted pepper into strips and set aside.

Bring a saucepan of water to the boil and cook the new potatoes for 10–15 minutes until they are soft when tested with the tip of a sharp knife. Drain well, return to the pan and place a clean tea towel over them to cool and really dry them out.

Bring a second saucepan of water to the boil and cook the lentils for 15–20 minutes until tender but still with a little bite and texture to them. Drain well and set aside.

Heat the remaining 2 tablespoons of olive oil in a frying pan over a medium heat, add the onion and cook, stirring, for 2 minutes.

When the potatoes are cool enough to handle, use your hands to break them up into chunky pieces, straight into the frying pan with the onion. Turn up the heat to high then add the butter. Leave the potatoes, without stirring, for a few minutes to get some lovely crispy edges to them, then toss them over to crisp up all over another 2 minutes.

Add the garlic, all of the spices and cooked lentils and cook, stirring, for another minute. Season with a good amount of salt. If the hash looks like it's drying out, add a little more butter or olive oil. When the hash is nice and crispy, fold the baby spinach and roast red pepper strips into the hash using a wooden spoon until it has all wilted.

Serve the hash, drizzled with yogurt and garnished with the mint leaves. For a more substantial offering you can also serve it with a crispy fried egg or a poached egg.

See pages 120–121 for the recipe photograph.

Food cultures all over the world have their own forms of dumpling, from sweet to savoury, steamed, poached or shallow-fried, like these wonderful gyozas. Dumpling-making is an art form, and the more you practise, the more skilled and proficient you'll become. You could serve these with just soy sauce, but roasted chilli oil is a heavenly condiment that will improve many dishes. Try stirring some through steamed rice or toss with egg noodles.

MUSHROOM & TEMPEH GYOZA

MAKES 20

1 teaspoon toasted sesame oil
4 tablespoons sunflower oil
150g shiitake mushrooms,
    finely chopped
100g Chinese cabbage,
    finely shredded
20g ginger, grated
2 garlic cloves, finely chopped
3 spring onions, finely chopped
50g tempeh, finely chopped
3 tablespoons soy sauce, plus
    extra to serve
2 teaspoons mirin
1–2 teaspoons cornflour
20 gyoza pastry wrappers
sea salt and freshly ground
    black pepper

TO SERVE
soy sauce
Roasted Chilli Oil (see page 90)

Heat the sesame oil and half the sunflower oil in a wok over a medium heat, add the mushrooms and cabbage and stir-fry for 2–3 minutes to soften. Add the ginger, garlic and spring onions and cook for a further 1–2 minutes.

Transfer the contents of the wok to a mixing bowl and add the tempeh, soy sauce and mirin, along with the cornflour to help bind the mix. Mix well and season with a little salt and pepper. Leave the gyoza filling to cool then chill in the fridge for 10–15 minutes.

Take the gyoza wrappers out of their packet and place a clean tea towel over them. Remove the gyoza filling from the fridge and, taking one wrapper at a time, place a heaped tablespoon of the filling in the centre of each wrapper.

Dip your finger in a small bowl of water then rub your wet finger around the outside of the gyoza wrapper. Fold the wrapper in half, crimping the edge 4–5 times to enclose the filling. Repeat with the remaining wrappers.

Heat 1cm of sunflower oil in a frying pan over a medium heat and begin to fry the gyozas, working in batches if needed. Cook each side of the gyozas for 1 minute, turning carefully, until golden brown. Remove with a slotted spoon and rest the gyoza on kitchen paper to drain off any excess oil. Serve with bowls of soy sauce and roasted chilli oil on the side.

See pages 124–125 for the recipe photograph.

Cabbage is so underrated. It's a hardy vegetable, so you can find a variety in season at almost any time of year. It's often thought of as something on the side or a 'filler' to a meal, but with some imagination and care it can really shine as the star of the show. Charring the cabbage gives it a little smokiness and sweetness from the caramelisation that takes place as it cooks. Miso butter gives it a wonderful salty and sweet flavour, and the togarashi gives it a cheeky peppery kick.

CHARRED HISPI CABBAGE
WITH MISO BUTTER & TOGARASHI

SERVES 4 AS A SIDE

40g unsalted butter, softened
1 tablespoon miso paste
2 tablespoons olive oil
1 large hispi cabbage, cut into 4 wedges with the core intact
¼ lemon, juice only
1 teaspoon sesame seeds
1–2 teaspoons togarashi spice mix (Japanese spice mix of sesame seeds, chilli, ginger, nori seaweed and sansho pepper)

Mix together the butter and miso in a small bowl and set aside.

Heat the olive oil in a frying pan over a high heat and cook the cabbage wedges cut-side down for 3–4 minutes until they are charred.

Lower the heat, add the miso butter and cook for a further 5 minutes, turning the wedges 2–3 times as they cook. Check the core of the cabbage using the tip of a sharp knife to make sure it is cooked through and tender.

Transfer the cabbage wedges to a plate and squeeze the lemon juice over them, then sprinkle with the sesame seeds and togarashi. The togarashi is quite spicy and peppery, so add to taste.

MasterChef Tip: *Try tossing some grilled or barbecued corn in the miso butter along with a sprinkling of the togarashi for a wonderful summer side dish.*

There is something heavenly about breaded fried food. The crunchy texture is just irresistible. The classic veal or chicken schnitzel gets the veg makeover here. To make a breaded dish show-stopping, the secret is always in the breadcrumbs. Make them fragrant and full of flavour. The possibilities are endless, but these are a great starting point. Coleslaw pairs delightfully with fried dishes, and adding yogurt to the coleslaw mix gives it freshness.

AUBERGINE SCHNITZEL
WITH FENNEL & CHILLI COLESLAW

SERVES 2

plain flour, to dust
1 egg, whisked
1 large aubergine, sliced into 4 steaks
sunflower oil, for shallow frying

FOR THE BREADCRUMBS
180g sourdough, crusts removed
5g flat-leaf parsley, finely chopped
1 teaspoon chopped thyme leaves
1 teaspoon chopped rosemary leaves
½ teaspoon chilli flakes
zest of ½ lemon
1 teaspoon sea salt
freshly ground black pepper

FOR THE COLESLAW
150g white cabbage, finely sliced
½ fennel bulb, finely sliced
2 spring onions, finely chopped
½ red chilli, deseeded and sliced into thin strips
5g flat-leaf parsley, roughly chopped
5g coriander, roughly chopped
50g mayonnaise
50g natural yogurt
juice of ¼ lemon
sea salt and freshly ground black pepper

Preheat the oven to 180°C Fan/200°C/Gas Mark 6.

Begin by making the breadcrumbs. Whizz the sourdough in a food processor until it forms fine crumbs. Transfer the breadcrumbs to a mixing bowl then add the remaining breadcrumb ingredients. Mix well and set aside.

For the coleslaw, combine all of the ingredients in a large bowl, mix well and season with salt and pepper.

Put the flour, whisked egg and prepared breadcrumbs into 3 separate shallow bowls. One aubergine steak at a time, first coat in flour, then dip in the egg, followed by the breadcrumbs and set aside on a plate until ready to cook.

Heat the sunflower oil in a frying pan over a medium to high heat. Once the oil is hot, begin frying the schnitzels. Cook for 2–3 minutes on each side until golden brown, working in batches if needed. Transfer the cooked schnitzels to a lined baking tray and transfer to the oven for 10–12 minutes.

Serve with the coleslaw, a side that's always pretty amazing with a schnitzel, and chips are optional!

Vegetable chilli 'con carne' is often the dish that first excites people new to vegetarian cooking, making them forget that there's no meat at all. A truly exceptional chilli should have real depth of flavour, layered with spices, herbs and a little heat. Try adding a grain for texture and a little bitterness from cocoa or a small amount of coffee to take your chilli to the next level. Then there's the accompaniments: add a few spoons of avocado and soured cream and then it really becomes something special.

VEGGIE CHILLI CON CARNE

SERVES 6–8

2 tablespoons olive oil
1 brown onion, finely chopped
1 small carrot, finely chopped
1 red pepper, chopped into
    1cm pieces
3 garlic cloves, finely chopped
½ tablespoon grated ginger
1 red chilli, finely chopped
1 teaspoon dried oregano
½ tablespoon chopped
    coriander stems
1 teaspoon chilli flakes
2 teaspoons ground coriander
1 teaspoon ground cumin
1 teaspoon smoked paprika
½ teaspoon ground cinnamon
200g freekeh (cracked wheat)
2 x 400g cans chopped tomatoes
1.5 litres vegetable stock
2 x 400g cans red kidney beans,
    drained
1 tablespoon cocoa nibs or
    dark cooking chocolate
handful coriander leaves
sea salt

TO SERVE
corn chips/tortillas
steamed rice
soured cream
smashed avocado
hot sauce

Heat the olive oil in a large heavy-based saucepan over a medium heat, add the onion and carrot and cook, stirring, for 2–3 minutes until they begin to soften. Add the red pepper, garlic, ginger and red chilli and cook for a further 1–2 minutes. Add the oregano, coriander stems, chilli flakes and the ground spices and cook for 30 seconds.

Add the freekeh along with the chopped tomatoes and vegetable stock then bring to the boil. Reduce the chilli con carne to a simmer and cook for 40–50 minutes until the freekeh is cooked and tender. If the chilli has dried out, add a little water to loosen it up.

Add the kidney beans and the cocoa nibs/cooking chocolate and cook for a further 2–3 minutes. Taste and season the chilli with a few pinches of sea salt then sprinkle over the coriander and serve with your favourite accompaniments.

Cooking is about finding balance, about combining elements that bring a dish together. Finding a harmonious mix of textures, temperatures and just the right level of saltiness, sweetness and sourness can bring joy to the taste buds. South East Asian cooks excel at building meals with contrasting yet balanced flavours. Nuoc cham dressing, a staple in Vietnamese cuisine, has a lovely balance of salty 'fish sauce', sourness from lime, a little heat from chilli and a bit of sugar to round it off.

ROASTED AUBERGINE
WITH MUSHROOMS & NUOC CHAM

SERVES 2

1 large aubergine, halved lengthways
2 tablespoons sunflower oil
½ red onion, finely chopped
½ tablespoon grated ginger
120g shiitake mushrooms, sliced
½ tablespoon light soy sauce
1 tablespoon unsalted peanuts, finely chopped
2 tablespoons panko breadcrumbs
olive oil, to drizzle

FOR THE NUOC CHAM DRESSING
1 tablespoon water
1 tablespoon vegetarian fish sauce
½ tablespoon lime juice
½ tablespoon rice vinegar
1 teaspoon caster sugar
1 small garlic clove, finely chopped
½ red chilli, deseeded and finely chopped

TO SERVE
steamed jasmine rice
coriander and mint leaves

Preheat the oven to 180°C Fan/200°C/Gas Mark 6.

To make the nuoc cham dressing, mix all of the ingredients in a bowl and set aside.

Scoop out the flesh from the aubergine, leaving a 5mm border of flesh around the skin to form two hollow shells. Roughly chop the aubergine flesh into 2cm pieces.

Heat the oil in a frying pan over a medium heat and cook the aubergine flesh, onion, ginger and mushrooms, stirring, for 5–7 minutes until soft. Season with the light soy sauce.

Fill the aubergine shells with the cooked vegetable mixture, put on an oven tray and roast in the oven for 20 minutes. After 20 minutes, scatter the peanuts over the top of the aubergine halves followed by the panko breadcrumbs then give the aubergines a little drizzle of oil. Roast for another 10 minutes until the breadcrumbs are crisp and golden.

Serve with steamed jasmine rice, with the coriander and mint leaves scattered over the top and the dressing on the side.

THOMAS FRAKE MASTERCHEF UK CHAMPION 2020

The Sunday roast dinner is a Great British favourite, but the vegetarian offering has often been pretty woeful, with dried nut roasts making regular appearances. I'm hoping to change this with my sage & onion chestnut roast – the perfect celebratory centrepiece for the vegetarian Sunday dinner table.

The familiar tastes of herbaceous sage and sweet onions are combined with the umami, almost meaty, flavours of mushrooms and yeast extract, making this something really special, and unlike those terrible nut roasts of the past. Dried cranberries and a tangy cranberry sauce add sweet and sour excitement to the dish, elevating this classic to *MasterChef* levels.

SAGE & ONION CHESTNUT ROAST
WITH CRANBERRY SAUCE

SERVES 4–6

50g dried cranberries
40g butter
2 white onions, very finely
    chopped or grated
2 parsnips, very finely chopped
    or grated
1 leek, very finely chopped
4 black garlic cloves, very finely
    chopped or mashed into
    a paste
150g chestnut mushrooms,
    chopped
zest of 1 orange
1 tablespoon chopped fresh sage
1 teaspoon dried thyme
1 tablespoon yeast extract
150g cooked chestnuts,
    finely chopped
100g walnuts, finely chopped
50g fresh brown breadcrumbs
100g cooked Puy lentils
50ml vegetable stock
2 eggs, beaten (or 100ml
    aquafaba – the liquid from
    a can of chickpeas)
sea salt and freshly ground
    black pepper

First make the cranberry sauce. Put the sugar, orange juice and port in a saucepan and bring to the boil. Add the cranberries, turn down the heat, and simmer for about 6 minutes until the cranberries are starting to break down. Frozen cranberries will take a little longer. Stir the mixture well, then transfer to a jar or container, and refrigerate for a few hours. It will thicken as it cools. This sauce is best made in advance and will keep for 7 days covered in the fridge.

Preheat the oven to 180°C Fan/200°C/Gas Mark 6. Line a metal 1kg loaf tin with baking parchment. Soak the dried cranberries in hot water for 5 minutes and then drain.

Heat 20g of the butter (or use olive oil if vegan) in a sauté pan over a medium heat. Add the finely chopped onions, parsnips, leek and black garlic to the pan and cook slowly over a low heat until softened and translucent, about 15 minutes, being careful not to burn them.

Add the chestnut mushrooms to the pan. Stir well and then cook them through until all the moisture in the mushrooms has fully evaporated, about 5 minutes. Add the orange zest, sage, thyme and yeast extract to the pan, cook for a couple of minutes more then remove the pan from the heat and allow to cool slightly.

Add the chestnuts, walnuts and breadcrumbs to the mushroom mixture with the Puy lentils, drained dried cranberries, vegetable stock and beaten eggs (or aquafaba if vegan). Season well with salt and pepper, stir the mixture thoroughly, then spoon into the lined loaf tin, pressing down gently.

FOR THE CRANBERRY SAUCE
100g light brown sugar
100ml fresh squeezed
    orange juice
25ml port
250g cranberries (fresh or frozen)

TO SERVE
gravy

Dot the top of the loaf with the remaining 20g of butter (or drizzle with 20ml olive oil if vegan). Cover the top with foil, and then roast in the oven for 30 minutes. Remove the foil and return to the oven for a further 20–30 minutes until the top is browned and the loaf is cooked through. This can be checked by inserting a skewer into the loaf, and if it comes out clean it will be ready. Remove the cooked loaf from the oven and leave to stand in the loaf tin for 20 minutes to rest.

Carefully remove the loaf from the tin and, using a knife if needed, carefully remove the baking paper from the cooked loaf. Leave to stand for 5 minutes before slicing into thick slices and serving with the cranberry sauce and lashings of gravy.

sustainability

Whatever the vegetable, a plate of tempura is a light and crispy delight. Choose vegetables that are local and in season for the tastiest results. If you can't get kecap manis, use dark soy sauce instead and add some sugar or honey to sweeten.

SEASONAL TEMPURA VEGETABLES
WITH SAMBAL KECAP

SERVES 4 AS A SNACK OR STARTER

sunflower or vegetable oil, for deep frying
4 mini aubergines, cut into thirds lengthways
10 asparagus spears, halved
8 spring onions, white part only (thinly slice green parts and reserve for the garnish)
½ courgette, cut into 5 x 1cm batons

FOR THE SAMBAL KECAP
3 tablespoons kecap manis (Indonesian sweet soy sauce)
2 shallots, finely chopped
2 red chillies, finely chopped

FOR THE TEMPURA BATTER
70g plain flour
30g rice flour
½ teaspoon sea salt
200ml sparkling water

If you have a deep-fat fryer, put the oil in it and set the temperature to 180°C. Otherwise, fill a large, heavy-based saucepan one-third full with the sunflower or vegetable oil. Heat until the oil reaches 180°C when tested on a food thermometer. The oil is hot enough when a small piece of bread dropped into it floats to the top and turns golden in 20 seconds.

Mix the sambal kecap ingredients in a bowl and set aside.

Make the tempura batter just before you are ready to fry the vegetables, so they will be nice and light and crispy. Mix the flour, rice flour and salt together in a medium bowl, then slowly add the sparkling water, whisking to form a batter.

Working in batches so as to not overcrowd the fryer or saucepan, dip the vegetables into the tempura batter then drop them into the hot oil. Using tongs, carefully move the vegetables around in the hot oil. The tempura vegetables are ready when they are floating and have started to turn golden, after 2–3 minutes. Remove with a slotted spoon and drain on kitchen paper. Keep warm.

Serve the tempura garnished with the reserved spring onion greens, with the sambal kecap alongside.

MasterChef Tip: *Always make a tempura batter just before you are ready to fry your vegetables for the lightest and crispiest results.*

See pages 140–141 for the recipe photograph.

A whole roasted cauliflower makes a delightful edible centrepiece that brings people together, like a classic roast does. Reducing meat consumption can have a dramatic positive impact on the environment, and swapping out that leg of roast lamb for a beautiful whole roasted cauliflower from time to time doesn't have to be a sacrifice with show-stoppers like this one.

WHOLE ROASTED CAULIFLOWER
WITH CORN PURÉE & TOMATILLO SALSA

SERVES 4

2 tablespoons olive oil
1 teaspoon sea salt
1 large cauliflower, with leaves removed and set aside
sesame seeds, to garnish

FOR THE CORN PURÉE
15g unsalted butter
1 shallot, chopped
½ garlic clove, chopped
2 cobs of corn, kernels removed
40ml water
10g vegetarian grating cheese, grated
1 tablespoon soured cream
sea salt and freshly ground black pepper

FOR THE TOMATILLO SALSA
10 canned tomatillos, drained
1 green chilli, chopped
25g coriander, chopped
juice of 1 lime
sea salt and freshly ground black pepper

Preheat the oven to 200°C Fan/220°C/Gas Mark 7.

Use your hands to massage the olive oil and salt into the whole cauliflower. Put the cauliflower in a roasting tin, transfer to the oven and roast for 50–60 minutes, until the edges are lovely and golden. Add the reserved cauliflower leaves to the roasting tin after 30 minutes and cook for the remaining cooking time until they are nice and crisp.

While the cauliflower is roasting, heat the butter in a saucepan over a medium heat then add the shallots and garlic. Cook, stirring, for 2 minutes then add the corn kernels and cook for another 3–4 minutes. Add the water and let simmer for a minute to finish cooking the corn.

Transfer the corn mixture to a blender, add the grated cheese and soured cream, blend to a rough purée then season with salt and pepper. Set aside and keep warm.

Clean the blender then add all of the ingredients for the tomatillo salsa and blend until smooth. Season to taste and set aside.

At the end of the roasting time, remove the cauliflower from the oven and let it stand for 5 minutes. Spread the corn purée over the base of a serving platter, top with the whole cauliflower, drizzle the tomatillo salsa over the top and garnish with the crispy leaves and sesame seeds.

Serve in the centre of the table and let everyone help themselves.

See pages 144–145 for the recipe photograph.

Food waste is an issue that all cooks need to be conscious of. Chefs have long highlighted the importance of using every part of an animal, and it is equally important not to waste often-discarded vegetable parts. That might mean using the leafy tops of carrots to make a pesto or, as in this gratin, using the green parts of leeks that would normally be binned to make a powder that provides a smoky barbecue-like flavour.

POTATO & LEEK GRATIN
WITH LEEK ASH

SERVES 4

butter, for greasing
300ml vegetable stock
450ml double cream
100ml milk
½ tablespoon Dijon mustard
30g vegetarian grating cheese, grated
1 teaspoon thyme leaves
2 bay leaves
2 garlic cloves, finely chopped
600g Maris Piper potatoes, washed and very finely sliced
60g mature Cheddar, grated
sea salt and freshly ground black pepper

FOR THE LEEK ASH
2–3 leeks, washed and white parts thinly sliced (reserve), green tops left whole

Preheat the oven to 180°C Fan/200°C/Gas Mark 6.

Begin by making the leek ash. Put the green parts of the leeks on a roasting tray and roast for 30 minutes until totally crisp and a very dark brown to black colour. Remove from the oven and leave to cool.

Once cool enough to handle, grind the blackened leek tops to a powder in a spice grinder. Store in a sealed container until needed. The leek ash recipe makes more than required but will keep for up to 2 weeks in a sealed container. Use as garnish on grilled vegetables for a smoky flavour.

For the gratin, lightly grease a deep-sided 24 x 18cm roasting tin or gratin dish with butter.

Whisk the vegetable stock, cream, milk, mustard and 15g of the vegetarian grated cheese in a saucepan and cook, stirring occasionally, over a medium heat until it just comes to the boil. Remove from the heat and add the thyme, bay leaves and garlic, season with salt and pepper then set aside to infuse for 15–20 minutes.

Arrange the sliced potato and sliced white leeks in layers in the baking tin/dish beginning with a layer of potato followed by a layer of leek, then repeat. Remove the bay leaves and then pour over the cream mixture and top the gratin with the Cheddar and remaining 15g vegetarian grated cheese.

Cover the baking tin/dish with foil and bake for 30 minutes. Remove the foil and bake for a further 30 minutes until lovely and golden. Remove from the oven and leave the gratin to rest for 10 minutes before serving.

Liberally sprinkle the leek ash over each serving of the gratin and serve with some fresh bitter leaves, such as mustard greens or rocket, drizzled with some good extra virgin olive oil.

LUCAS FURTADO MASTERCHEF BRAZIL CONTESTANT 2015

Mushrooms grow abundantly in much of the world. Edible and medicinal, they provide high-quality protein that can be produced with greater biological efficiency than animal protein. They are rich in fibre, minerals and vitamins and have a low total fat content, with a high proportion of polyunsaturated fatty acids. Many species also have tonic and medicinal properties, and their texture, aroma and flavour are attractive to the human palate. They grow all over the world, and are incredibly sustainable.

In Brazil, mushroom consumption has increased significantly in recent years and they have more space on restaurant menus. Veganism and vegetarianism have increased considerably, and mushrooms are sources of protein for these groups. This simple soup is a great way to showcase them.

MUSHROOM SOUP

SERVES 2

150g king oyster mushrooms
100g white button mushrooms
50g shiitake mushrooms
50g portobello mushrooms
50g butter, plus 1–2 teaspoons
    extra
1 leek with root attached, sliced
    and roots reserved for optional
    garnish
3 garlic cloves, crushed
thyme leaves, to taste
50ml brandy
150ml milk
200ml double cream
sea salt and freshly ground
    black pepper

Clean the mushrooms using a clean cloth and then cut them into even cubes. Set aside 25g of the cubed portobello mushrooms for the garnish.

Melt the 50g butter in a saucepan over a low heat, then add the leek and crushed garlic. Cook, stirring, until the garlic starts to brown (2–3 minutes), then add the mushrooms and thyme. Cook, stirring, until the mushrooms are soft.

When the mushrooms are soft, add the brandy and cook over a medium heat to evaporate some of the alcohol.

Add the milk and the cream to the pan and cook, stirring, for 10 minutes.

Blend the soup using a hand-held blender until smooth but with some chunks remaining.

Return the soup to the pan, season as required and cook for 5 minutes to thicken. While the soup is thickening, heat the 1–2 teaspoons of butter in a frying pan. When hot, add the reserved portobello mushrooms and cook, stirring, until browned. Set aside and, if using the leek roots, use the remaining butter to fry the leek roots until golden.

To serve, pour the soup into deep bowls and decorate with the reserved and fried mushrooms and leek roots.

Some vegetables are more sustainable than others. Vast amounts of water and energy are required to produce certain fruits and vegetables and some factory-produced meat substitutes. Where possible, buy organic vegetables but also think about using vegetables that are less resource-intensive. Root vegetables are a wonderful choice, and often-overlooked celeriac is brilliant roasted or grilled in large pieces to really bring out its peppery flavour and robust texture.

CELERIAC STEAKS
WITH CHIMICHURRI & APPLE CHILLI COLESLAW

SERVES 4

**1 large celeriac, cut into
    1.5–2cm steaks**
2 tablespoons olive oil
2 teaspoons sea salt flakes
**sea salt and freshly ground
    black pepper**

FOR THE CHIMICHURRI
**25g coriander leaves, finely
    chopped**
**25g flat-leaf parsley, finely
    chopped**
4 spring onions, finely chopped
2 garlic cloves, finely chopped
**1 jalapeño chilli, deseeded and
    finely chopped**
2 teaspoons dried oregano
2½ tablespoons rice vinegar
100ml extra virgin olive oil
2 teaspoons sea salt

FOR THE APPLE CHILLI COLESLAW
**350g white cabbage, finely
    shredded**
150g carrot, cut into thin strips
1 small red onion, finely sliced
**1 Granny Smith apple, peeled,
    cored and cut into thin strips**
**1 red chilli, deseeded and cut into
    thin strips**
80g mayonnaise
80g soured cream
1 tablespoon lemon juice

Preheat the oven to 180°C Fan/200°C/Gas Mark 6.

Line a baking tray with baking parchment and put the celeriac steaks on the tray in a single layer. Drizzle with the olive oil on both sides and season with the sea salt flakes. Give each steak a good season with freshly cracked black pepper then transfer to the oven and roast for 20 minutes. After 20 minutes, carefully turn the steaks over and roast for another 20 minutes until golden and crisp.

While the celeriac steaks are in the oven, combine all the chimichurri ingredients in a bowl and mix well.

For the apple chilli coleslaw, combine all the ingredients in a large bowl and season well with salt and pepper.

Serve the celeriac steaks drizzled with the chimichurri sauce, with the apple chilli coleslaw alongside.

The classic British leftovers dish. A traditional favourite that makes use of whatever's lying around and needs using up gets a little makeover in this recipe. With just a bit of extra work you can turn it into a refreshing and refined weekend brunch with light and contrasting flavours. One of the glorious things about bubble and squeak is that it's not a static recipe, so can be adjusted depending on what you have to use up.

BUBBLE & SQUEAK
WITH ROAST AUBERGINE PURÉE, HERBED YOGURT
& QUICK-PICKLED SHALLOTS

SERVES 4

4 tablespoons olive oil
2 leeks, washed and sliced
½ teaspoon crushed fennel seeds
1 teaspoon chopped thyme leaves
500g Savoy cabbage, sliced
**1kg potatoes, peeled, steamed
    and mashed**
**2 tablespoons chopped
    flat-leaf parsley**
plain flour, for dusting
rocket leaves, to serve
**sea salt and freshly ground
    black pepper**

FOR THE QUICK-PICKLED SHALLOTS
200ml cider vinegar
50ml water
60g caster sugar
2 teaspoons sea salt
6 black peppercorns
200g shallots, peeled and sliced

FOR THE ROAST AUBERGINE PURÉE
2 aubergines, halved lengthways
2 tablespoons olive oil
juice of ½ lemon

FOR THE HERBED YOGURT
200ml natural yogurt
2 tablespoons chopped coriander
**2 tablespoons chopped
    flat-leaf parsley**
½ tablespoon chopped dill

Preheat the oven to 180°C Fan/200°C/Gas Mark 6.

For the quick-pickled shallots, bring the cider vinegar and water to the boil then add the sugar, salt and peppercorns. Add the shallots, boil for 1 minute, remove from the heat and leave to cool. Transfer to a sterilised jar and store until needed.

Next make the aubergine purée. Place the halved aubergines on a roasting tray, drizzle with the olive oil and season with salt and pepper. Roast for 40 minutes until the flesh is tender. When cool enough to handle, use a spoon to scrape the flesh into a mixing bowl (discard the skins). Mash the flesh, add the lemon juice and taste to see if more salt and pepper is needed. Set aside.

For the bubble and squeak, heat 2 tablespoons of the olive oil in a frying pan over a medium heat and cook the leeks, stirring, for 2–3 minutes until soft. Add the fennel seeds, thyme and the Savoy cabbage and cook until the cabbage is soft. Remove from the heat and add to the mashed potato and the parsley, then season with salt and pepper.

When cool enough to handle, shape the mixture into 8 equal patties. Give each patty a dusting of flour, put on a lined baking tray and chill in the fridge for 15–20 minutes to firm up.

Heat the remaining 2 tablespoons of olive oil in a frying pan over a medium heat, add the bubble and squeak patties and cook until golden brown on all sides and heated through (you may need to do this in batches depending on the size of your frying pan; keep the cooked patties warm).

For the herbed yogurt dressing, whizz all the ingredients in a blender until smooth then set aside.

To serve, spoon some roast aubergine purée onto each plate followed by 2 of the bubble patties. Place a small handful of rocket on each plate, drizzle with the yogurt dressing and finish with the quick-pickled shallots.

Two ways to cook more sustainably are to buy less (particularly things that are pre-made) and make more (from scratch). There are so many wonderful artisan food producers but it's satisfying and rewarding to make things yourself, such as a basic fresh cheese or homemade pasta. It helps the environment by cutting down on single-use packaging and by reducing transport costs and overall carbon footprint. But the greatest part? You have the joy of gaining and perfecting a new skill using your own bare hands.

MUSHROOM TORTELLINI
WITH 'DIY' RICOTTA, PEAS & PINE NUTS

SERVES 2

FOR THE RICOTTA
1 litre organic whole milk
good pinch of sea salt
2 tablespoons cider vinegar

FOR THE FILLING
1 tablespoon olive oil
200g portobello mushrooms, finely chopped
2 spring onions, finely chopped
1 garlic clove, finely chopped
1 teaspoon finely chopped rosemary
finely grated zest of ½ lemon
100g ricotta (from recipe above; use the leftover ricotta in another recipe)
sea salt and freshly ground black pepper

FOR THE TORTELLINI PASTA
165g '00' pasta flour, plus extra to dust
pinch of sea salt
2 eggs, beaten

FOR THE SAUCE
2 tablespoons extra virgin olive oil
1 tablespoon unsalted butter
100g frozen peas, defrosted

To make the ricotta, put the milk and salt in a heavy-based saucepan and slowly bring the milk up to 95 degrees. Use a thermometer to check the temperature. Remove from the heat, add the vinegar and stir continuously for 1–2 minutes. Leave to cool and rest for 15 minutes.

Use a slotted spoon to remove the solid curds that have formed in the milk. Place the curds in a muslin cloth or a clean kitchen towel, put inside a fine sieve, suspend the sieve over a bowl to catch the liquid then put in the fridge (discard the whey or use in soups or to make bread). Let the ricotta stand in the fridge for at least 2 hours before using. The longer it is left to stand the firmer it will become. At this stage, the ricotta will last up to 3 days in a container in the fridge.

To make the filling, heat the olive oil in a frying pan over a medium heat and cook the mushrooms, spring onions, garlic and rosemary for 3–4 minutes until the mushrooms are nice and soft. Remove from the heat, add the lemon zest and season with salt and pepper. Set aside in a large bowl to cool. When cool, add the ricotta to the bowl and mix well.

Now to make your pasta. Put the flour in a heap on a clean work surface, mix in the salt and then make a well in the centre. Pour the beaten eggs into the well and, using your hands, bring the flour and eggs together in the centre. Knead to form a smooth dough. If it is slightly too wet, add a little extra flour.

Transfer the dough to a lightly floured bowl, cover and leave in the fridge to stand for 15 minutes.

Roll the pasta dough through a pasta machine, starting with the widest setting and finishing on the thinnest. Using a 9cm cutter, cut out 14 circles. You will need to re-roll the offcuts and put the dough back through the pasta machine to obtain all 14 circles.

Lay the circles out on a dusted work surface. Place a heaped teaspoon of the filling into the centre of each pasta circle. Using wet fingers, fold the pasta over to make a half-moon shape, then fold it again, making sure to stick the tortellini well together to encase the filling. Put the tortellini on a lightly floured plate and chill in the fridge for 30 minutes.

TO SERVE
8 basil leaves, torn
1 tablespoon toasted pine nuts
vegetarian grating cheese,
   grated, to serve

Bring a saucepan of salted water to the boil. For the sauce, heat the extra virgin olive oil and the butter in a large frying pan over a low heat, toss in the peas then set aside. When the water has come to the boil, carefully add the tortellini and cook for 4–5 minutes, until they float to the surface.

Remove the tortellini using a slotted spoon and transfer to the frying pan with the peas. Add a tablespoon or two of the pasta cooking water and toss the pasta and peas well to combine. Season with salt and pepper.

Serve the tortellini with the basil leaves, pine nuts and the grated cheese scattered over the top.

MasterChef Tip: *The ricotta will make more than needed, but it is also lovely served on some grilled sourdough with figs and a drizzle of honey.*

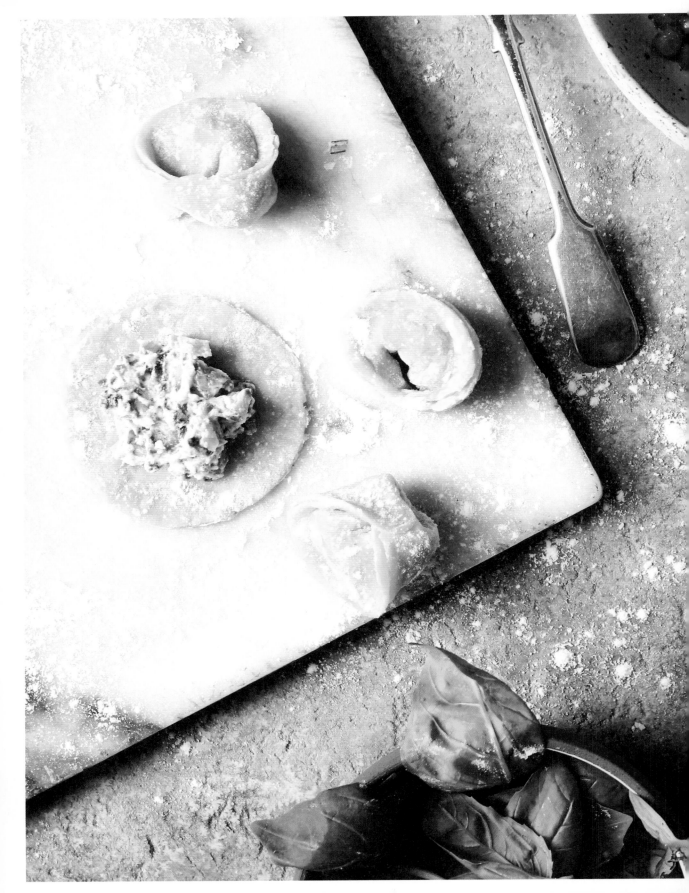

In autumn and winter, big, hearty, warming dishes are physically and mentally nourishing. A rich, meaty ragù is always welcome but with many people looking to reduce their meat consumption, it's good to know there are plenty of wonderful meat-free comfort options for the colder months. This dish is wonderfully wholesome, creamy and will certainly warm you on a chilly evening. You can braise other seasonal vegetables in place of cabbage; mushrooms work exceptionally well as a meat substitute.

BRAISED CABBAGE & KALE
WITH RICOTTA POLENTA

SERVES 4

1 tablespoon olive oil
1 brown onion, finely sliced
2 garlic cloves, finely chopped
1 hispi cabbage, cored and cut
    into rough chunks
1 tablespoon unsalted butter
1 teaspoon fennel seeds
½ teaspoon chilli flakes
60g kale, shredded
1 tablespoon cider vinegar
2 tablespoons almonds, toasted
    and roughly chopped
sourdough toast, to serve

FOR THE POLENTA
600ml vegetable stock
120g polenta
80g ricotta
20g vegetarian grating cheese,
    grated
12g basil leaves, sliced
sea salt and freshly ground
    black pepper

First prepare the polenta. Bring the vegetable stock to the boil in a large saucepan and add the polenta. Reduce to a simmer and cook for 8–10 minutes, stirring constantly until thickened. Add the ricotta, grated cheese and basil, season with salt and pepper and stir well. If the polenta is a little too thick, thin out with a little more vegetable stock or water. Set aside and keep warm.

For the cabbage and kale, heat the olive oil in a frying pan over a medium heat, add the onion and garlic and cook, stirring, for 2–3 minutes until soft. Add the cabbage, butter, fennel seeds and chilli flakes and cook for 5–7 minutes, stirring. The cabbage should still retain a little bite to it. Add the kale and vinegar and cook for another minute.

Serve the polenta topped with the cabbage and kale, sprinkled with the toasted almonds, with toasted sourdough.

Jackfruit is becoming a more popular ingredient in vegetarian and plant-based cooking for good reason. The fruit itself is the largest tree-borne fruit in the world and each tree yields plenty of fruit – but the truly sustainable part of jackfruit is that it does not require additional resource-draining irrigation systems. It also promotes regenerative ecosystems because it can be inter-grown with other crops. This aromatic curry, with deep-fried nuggets of jackfruit, celebrates a sustainable fruit that's easy to enjoy.

'SFJ' SOUTHERN FRIED JACKFRUIT
WITH LEMONGRASS COCONUT CURRY

SERVES 2

1 can young jackfruit (in water), drained
125ml buttermilk
sunflower oil, for deep frying
steamed rice, to serve
sea salt and freshly ground black pepper

FOR THE LEMONGRASS COCONUT CURRY

1½ tablespoons sunflower oil
2 shallots, finely chopped
2 garlic cloves, finely chopped
1 lemongrass stalk (white part only), finely chopped
1 green chilli, finely chopped
½ tablespoon curry powder
1 teaspoon ground turmeric
pinch of chilli flakes
1½ tablespoons vegetarian fish sauce or soy sauce
1 tablespoon granulated sugar
300ml coconut milk
squeeze of lime juice

FOR THE FLOUR COATING

120g plain flour
80g rice flour
2 teaspoons baking powder
1 teaspoon sea salt
1 teaspoon freshly ground black pepper
½ teaspoon cayenne pepper
½ teaspoon onion powder

Begin by making the curry sauce. Heat the sunflower oil in a saucepan over a medium heat and cook the shallots until soft, for 2 minutes. Add the garlic, lemongrass and green chilli and cook for a further minute. Add the curry powder, turmeric and chilli flakes along with the vegetarian fish sauce/soy sauce and sugar. Stir to dissolve the sugar, then add the coconut milk.

Bring the curry sauce to the boil, reduce the heat and simmer for 15–20 minutes, until the sauce has thickened slightly. Add a couple of squeezes of lime juice to balance the flavour and set aside.

Trim away any tough, stalk-like parts from the drained jackfruit (discard). Put the prepared jackfruit in a bowl with the buttermilk and season with salt and pepper. In a separate, shallow bowl, mix all of the flour coating ingredients together.

If you have a deep-fat fryer, put the sunflower oil in it and set the temperature to 180°C. Otherwise, fill a large, heavy-based saucepan one-third full with the oil. Heat until the oil reaches 180°C when tested on a food thermometer. The oil is hot enough when a small piece of bread dropped into it floats to the top and turns golden in 20 seconds.

You can now begin to coat the jackfruit. One piece at a time, roll the marinated jackfruit in the flour coating, making sure to work the coating well into the jackfruit. Repeat the process. Do the same with the remaining jackfruit, until all of it has been double-coated in the flour mixture.

Carefully lower the coated jackfruit pieces into the hot oil in the fryer/saucepan using a slotted spoon. You can do this in 2 batches to ensure the oil remains at the high temperature needed.

Fry the jackfruit pieces for 3–4 minutes until they are lovely and golden. Using a slotted spoon, remove from the oil and drain on kitchen paper. Leave to rest for 5 minutes before serving.

While the jackfruit is resting, reheat the curry sauce. Ladle the curry sauce into bowls and place the fried jackfruit on top. Serve with plenty of steamed rice.

Abundant with nutrients, buddha bowls (or hippie or macro bowls) are sunshine and goodness – the sort of thing served in warm, coastal beachside cafés across the world. These are the perfect tonic for those wanting to better fuel the body and look after their health in a fast-paced, digital world. The joy of a buddha bowl is that there is no set recipe. Think of it like layering a colourful painting. The only guideline is to use a variety of grains and pulses and an array of seasonal vegetables, topped with nuts and seeds for added texture and nutrients.

BUDDHA BOWLS
WITH TAHINI GREEN GODDESS DRESSING & SOY ALMONDS

SERVES 4

200g pearl barley
250g tenderstem broccoli,
  spears cut in half
300g red cabbage, finely
  shredded
1 medium carrot, cut into thin
  matchsticks
2 avocados, sliced
extra virgin olive oil
toasted sesame seeds, to garnish
sea salt and freshly ground
  black pepper

FOR THE SOY ALMONDS
3 tablespoons almonds, skin on
1 tablespoon soy sauce

FOR THE TAHINI GREEN GODDESS
  DRESSING
15g coriander leaves
15g basil leaves
15g flat-leaf parsley leaves
1 garlic clove, roughly chopped
2 spring onions, roughly chopped
½ tablespoon tahini
1 tablespoon lemon juice
1 tablespoon extra virgin olive oil
240g Greek yogurt

Preheat the oven to 180°C Fan/200°C/Gas Mark 6.

For the soy almonds, mix together the almonds and soy sauce, put on a baking tray and roast in the oven for 7–8 minutes until they are nice and golden. Set aside.

Rinse the pearl barley in cold water for 1 minute then drain. Put the pearl barley in a saucepan of salted cold water and bring to the boil. Reduce the heat to a simmer and cook for 20 minutes until the barley is tender. Drain and set aside to cool.

While the pearl barley is cooking, blanch the broccoli in a saucepan of salted boiling water for 60–90 seconds. Drain immediately and run cold water over the broccoli to stop it cooking any further.

Whizz all the ingredients for the tahini green goddess dressing in a blender until smooth and with a vibrant green colour. Season with salt and pepper and set aside.

Begin building the buddha bowls by placing the pearl barley into each bowl first with a small drizzle of extra virgin olive oil. Add the cabbage, carrot and broccoli as separate components around the bowl. Place half a sliced avocado on top of the salad and then dress the salad with some of the tahini green goddess dressing.

Garnish with the soy almonds and toasted sesame seeds and serve the remaining dressing on the side.

MasterChef Tip: *If you're looking for an added nutritional benefit, try serving the buddha bowls with 1–2 tablespoons of unpasteurised apple cider vinegar on the side. It is full of healthy bacteria to support a healthy immune system.*

SIMON TOOHEY MASTERCHEF AUSTRALIA FINALIST 2019

Beetroot has to be one of my favourite vegetables. It grows in the autumn and winter months, produces a variety of astonishing colours and patterns, and is extremely versatile. Its history goes back to the mid-1500s and it played a massive hand in the world of distillation, especially in Dutch-style gins.

A lot of people don't really know what to do with the whole beetroot. As with cauliflower and broccoli, there is so much more that we can do by using the whole ingredient. If you cannot get beetroots with their leaves attached, you can make the salad with just the stalks too. Here is a dish that I love to cook.

BEETROOT GLAZED IN SOY
WITH CRISPED LEAVES, PICKLED STEM SALAD & CREAMY POLENTA

SERVES 4

6 medium beetroot, leaves on
pinch of sea salt
drizzle of olive oil
2 tablespoons light soy sauce
sea salt and freshly ground
    black pepper

FOR THE PICKLED STEM SALAD
100ml apple cider vinegar
60g caster sugar
1 teaspoon sea salt
2 handfuls rocket leaves
25g hazelnuts, roasted
30 vegan feta (or regular feta)

FOR THE POLENTA
300ml oat milk
300ml vegetable stock
200g polenta
50g vegan butter (or regular
    butter)

Preheat the oven to 200°C Fan/220°C/Gas Mark 7.

For the beetroot, cut the stems off where they connect with the bulb. Wearing kitchen gloves if you like, to prevent your hands staining, wash both stem and root in water until any dirt is removed. Sprinkle 4 of the beetroot with salt, drizzle with olive oil and wrap in baking parchment and then foil (never wrap with just foil as it can leave a metallic taste).

Roast the wrapped beetroot in the oven for 40 minutes, or until a skewer inserted into the centre comes out smoothly. Leave to cool slightly, then squeeze gently and peel the skin off the beetroot. This will be super-easy – it will just slide off.

Juice the other 2 beetroots in a juicer. If you don't have a juicer, blend them to a purée. If you are blending them, once they have reached a purée consistency, you can either squeeze the juice out by wrapping the pulp in a clean piece of muslin and squeezing the juice into a bowl, or just use the pulped beetroot. The flavour will be the same; there will just be a slightly different texture at the end. Set aside until ready to serve.

Pour the juice or purée into a saucepan over a high heat, add the soy sauce, bring to the boil then reduce the heat so the liquid is at a simmer. Reduce until there is about 4 tablespoons of liquid left. It should be rich, sweet and salty.

For the pickled beetroot stem salad, put the apple cider vinegar, sugar and salt in a saucepan and bring to the boil.

In the meantime, cut the stems from the beetroot leaves (keep the leaves), chop the stems to 2.5cm lengths and put them in a heatproof bowl. Once the sugar has melted in the pickling liquid, pour the liquid over the stems and leave to sit for 30 minutes.

Wash the rocket, roughly chop the nuts, break up the feta and put them all in a serving bowl. Strain the beetroot stems from the pickling liquid (reserve the liquid), and add the stems to the salad ingredients.

For the polenta, put the oat milk and most of the stock in a large pan over a medium heat and bring to a simmer. Slowly rain in the polenta, whisking at the same time. Keep stirring until the polenta is soft and cooked through. (Follow the cooking instructions on the packet for timing, as instant and non-instant polenta have different cooking times.) If the polenta is getting too thick, add some more stock. Once cooked, turn off the heat and whisk in the butter.

To make the beetroot crips, turn the oven temperature down to 100°C Fan/120°C /Gas Mark ½ and leave the oven door slightly ajar to let the oven cool slightly.

Put the beetroot leaves on a baking tray lined with baking parchment. Brush or spray the leaves with a little olive oil, sprinkle with salt and pepper and cook in the oven until nice and crisp, about 15 minutes.

To serve, spoon a generous amount of creamy polenta into each bowl, chop the roasted beetroot into quarters and layer on top. Put a small handful of salad on top of the beetroot, drizzle the beetroot and soy dressing around and finish with the beetroot crisps.

All hail the kiev. It's a midweek staple, but there's no need to do without this weekly go-to dish if you're reducing your meat consumption. One of the joys of cooking more vegetarian dishes is the increased amount of learning and creativity that can be achieved, along with impressing our family and friends with newfound dishes – like this meatless kiev.

MUSHROOM KIEVS
WITH THAI BASIL & CHILLI COLESLAW

SERVES 4

50g butter, at room temp
1 large garlic clove, finely chopped
4 tablespoons chopped flat-leaf parsley
150g baking potatoes, peeled and chopped into chunks
150g chestnut mushrooms, finely chopped
4 tablespoons olive oil
2 sprigs rosemary leaves, finely chopped
½ teaspoon chopped thyme leaves
100g canned lentils, drained
15g sesame seeds, toasted
4 tablespoons plain flour
1 egg, lightly beaten
200g sourdough breadcrumbs
sea salt and freshly ground black pepper

FOR THE THAI BASIL & CHILLI COLESLAW
1 green chilli, roughly chopped
25g Thai basil
160g crème fraîche
160g mayonnaise
400g Savoy cabbage, finely shredded
4 spring onions, sliced into rounds
12g coriander leaves
30g rocket leaves

Begin by making the garlic and parsley butter for the kievs. Mix the butter, garlic and half of the parsley in a small bowl, cover and chill in the fridge until needed.

For the coleslaw dressing, whizz the green chilli, Thai basil, crème fraîche and mayonnaise in a blender until smooth. Cover and chill in the fridge until needed.

For the kievs, steam the potatoes for 10 minutes until they are soft and tender. Mash by hand, season with salt and pepper then set aside to cool.

While the mash is cooling, heat a saucepan over a medium heat and cook the mushrooms in half the olive oil with the rosemary and thyme for 5 minutes until they are soft. Add the mushroom mixture to the mashed potatoes along with the lentils, sesame seeds and remaining parsley.

Once cool enough to handle, shape the kiev mixture into 4 equal balls. Using your thumb, make an indentation into each one and insert ½ tablespoon of the garlic butter. Form the mixture around the garlic butter to enclose it, and work into a kiev shape. Repeat to form 4 kievs.

To crumb the kievs, put the flour, beaten egg and breadcrumbs into 3 separate shallow bowls. Dip each kiev in flour first followed by the beaten egg and finally the breadcrumbs. Put the 4 crumbed kievs on a plate then chill in the fridge for 30 minutes to firm up.

Preheat the oven to 180°C Fan/200°C/Gas Mark 6. Heat the remaining olive oil in a frying pan over a medium heat. When hot, fry each kiev until golden brown on all sides for 5 minutes, taking care not to break them. Put on a baking tray and bake in the oven for 15–20 minutes.

While the kievs are baking, finish the coleslaw. Mix the coleslaw dressing in a large bowl with the cabbage, spring onions, coriander and rocket. Serve the kievs with the coleslaw on the side.

Laksa is a coconut and curry-based rice noodle soup from South East Asia that's particularly popular in Malaysia and Singapore. Laksa is as enjoyable on a warm, sun-filled day as it is in the depths of a dark winter evening. This vegetarian version is also 'local' – it's made using native vegetables to help reduce food miles.

BRUSSELS SPROUT & HISPI CABBAGE LAKSA
WITH TOFU PUFFS

SERVES 4

400g medium rice noodles
60ml sunflower oil, plus extra
    for shallow frying
1 small aubergine, cut into
    1cm pieces
400ml can coconut milk
800ml vegetable stock
1 tablespoon caster sugar
100g hispi cabbage, finely
    shredded
10 Brussels sprouts
270g firm tofu, cut into
    1cm pieces
1½ tablespoons soy sauce
cornflour, for dusting
coriander sprigs, lime wedges
    and chopped chilli, to serve
sea salt

FOR THE LAKSA PASTE
1 brown onion, chopped
2 garlic cloves, chopped
4cm piece ginger, peeled and
    chopped
5 red chillies, deseeded and
    chopped
1 teaspoon ground turmeric
2 teaspoons ground coriander
1 tablespoon chopped
    coriander stalks
1 tablespoon soy sauce
2 tablespoons water

Cook the rice noodles according to packet instructions, drain and set aside.

Put all the ingredients for the laksa paste in a blender and blend until smooth.

Heat the 60ml sunflower oil in a large saucepan over a medium heat and cook the aubergine pieces for 2–3 minutes until they start to soften and break down. Using a slotted spoon, transfer the aubergine to a plate lined with kitchen paper to drain, keeping the oil in the pan.

Put the laksa paste in the saucepan with the leftover oil from the aubergines and cook for 3–5 minutes over a medium heat, stirring regularly.

Add the coconut milk and vegetable stock and bring to the boil. Add the sugar, stir well, then turn down the heat to a simmer and cook for 15 minutes. Add the cabbage, Brussels sprouts and aubergine and cook for a further 2–3 minutes until the vegetables have softened. Taste and add a little salt if needed.

Dress the tofu in the soy sauce. Put the cornflour in a shallow bowl then dip the tofu pieces in the cornflour. Heat 5mm of sunflower in a frying pan over a medium to high heat then cook the tofu for 2–3 minutes, turning carefully, until the tofu is lovely and golden and crisp. Remove with a slotted spoon and drain on a plate lined with kitchen paper.

Divide the noodles among 4 deep bowls and ladle in the laksa soup. Top with the fried tofu and garnish with a few sprigs of coriander. Serve with lime wedges and freshly chopped chilli for those who enjoy their laksa with a real kick.

This gnocchi recipe is a great example of how to use an entire vegetable without letting anything go to waste – the skin and seeds are used, as well as the flesh. One method is to roast it with the skin on, allowing the skin to soften as it roasts. Or, as in this recipe, use the peeled skin to make crunchy crisps for added texture. Wash and toast the seeds, then use them in salads or muesli. Here, I suggest sprinkling them on top of the gnocchi as you would with pine nuts, for a crunchy finishing touch.

BUTTERNUT SQUASH GNOCCHI
WITH SAGE, TOMATO & PUMPKIN CRISPS

SERVES 4

250g butternut squash, peeled (peel reserved), flesh cut into 1cm pieces
1 tablespoon olive oil
450g Maris Piper potatoes, peeled
15g unsalted butter
100g plain flour, plus extra to dust
2 tablespoons extra virgin olive oil
8 sage leaves, finely sliced
250ml Classic Tomato Sauce (page 180)
sea salt and freshly ground black pepper

TO SERVE

vegetarian grating cheese, grated
finely chopped flat-leaf parsley

Preheat the oven to 180°C Fan/200°C/Gas Mark 6. Put the butternut squash pieces and the butternut peel on two separate baking trays and drizzle with the olive oil. Roast the peel (for the crisps) for 10 minutes until dark golden and crisp. Roast the butternut squash for 25 minutes until soft, then set aside.

Put the potatoes in a saucepan of cold water, bring to the boil, then reduce the heat and simmer for 25–30 minutes until they are just soft enough to pierce with the tip of a sharp knife. Drain, return them to the saucepan and put the pan over a low heat for 2–3 minutes to really dry out the potatoes.

Pass the potatoes and the butternut squash through a potato ricer into a mixing bowl. (If you don't have a potato ricer, you can mash them by hand but be sure to mash really well, leaving no lumps.) Add the butter to the mixture then add the flour in a couple of batches, stirring to combine between additions, to form a dough. Season with salt and cracked pepper.

Once the dough has come together, turn it out onto a lightly floured work surface. Divide the dough into 4 equal pieces then gently roll each into 2cm-wide logs. Using a sharp knife, cut the logs into 2cm pieces and put on a lightly floured tray. Chill the gnocchi in the fridge for 30 minutes.

Bring a large saucepan of salted water to the boil. While the water is coming to the boil, heat the olive oil in a frying pan over a medium heat then fry the sage leaves for 1–2 minutes. Add the tomato sauce, stir, and set aside.

Cook the gnocchi for 3–4 minutes in the boiling water. When they float to the surface, remove them using a slotted spoon and add to the frying pan with the tomato sauce and sage. Toss the gnocchi well to combine. Serve with grated cheese, parsley and the pumpkin crisps scattered over the top.

Sea vegetables like dulse and samphire are great to eat for their health benefits, and for their sustainability. Roughly 70 per cent of the earth's surface is ocean, yet 'sea vegetables' go relatively underused. Because they don't require irrigation, valuable freshwater resources aren't needed. Plus, they grow at a much quicker rate than vegetables grown on land. You could think of it as pasta for the planet.

SPAGHETTI WITH DULSE & SAMPHIRE

SERVES 2

250g spaghetti
1 tablespoon olive oil
15g butter, plus extra (optional)
1 shallot, finely chopped
1 garlic clove, finely chopped
½ red chilli, finely chopped
100ml dry white wine
1½ tablespoons dulse (dried red seaweed)
100g samphire (or 6 asparagus spears, finely sliced)
1 small handful flat-leaf parsley, finely chopped
sea salt and freshly ground black pepper

TO SERVE
vegetarian grating cheese, grated
lemon wedges

Cook the spaghetti in salted water following the instructions on the packet. When draining the spaghetti, keep some of the pasta water (you will need around 50ml).

Heat the olive oil and the butter in a frying pan over a medium heat, add the shallot, garlic and chilli and cook, stirring, for 1 minute. Add the white wine and cook for 30 seconds then add the reserved pasta water, dulse and samphire. Bring to the boil then add the cooked spaghetti.

Add the parsley and toss to combine everything a few times, making sure that the spaghetti is heated through and nicely coated. If it seems a little dry, add a little more butter. Season with salt and freshly cracked black pepper and serve immediately with freshly grated cheese and lemon wedges on the side.

One of the most comforting dishes is the delight that is lasagne. With its wonderful richness and creamy goodness, it's a firm staple in autumn and winter. There are plenty of options available using just vegetables to deliver that same feeling of warmth and comfort. The combination of mushrooms and lentils provides this perfectly, and using a variety of mushrooms adds to the textural experience. Just as you would cook a beef ragù sauce 'low and slow', use the same method here with the mushroom and lentil ragù to let it develop a beautiful deep, rich flavour.

MUSHROOM & LENTIL LASAGNE

SERVES 6–8

1 tablespoon olive oil
1 brown onion, finely chopped
1 small carrot, finely chopped
1 celery stick, finely chopped
2 garlic cloves, finely chopped
2 bay leaves
½ teaspoon chilli flakes
125ml red wine
350g mixed mushrooms, very finely chopped
500ml Classic Tomato Sauce (see page 180) or canned chopped tomatoes
600ml vegetable stock
6g basil leaves, torn
1 tablespoon roughly chopped flat-leaf parsley
250g cooked puy lentils
sea salt and freshly ground black pepper

FOR THE BÉCHAMEL SAUCE
60g unsalted butter
60g plain flour
1 litre whole milk
1 bay leaf
½ teaspoon freshly grated nutmeg
1 teaspoon Dijon mustard
50g vegetarian grating cheese, grated

To make the ragù, heat the olive oil in a heavy-based saucepan over a low to medium heat and slowly cook the onion, carrot, celery and garlic for 10 minutes until the vegetables are soft and sweet. Add the bay leaves and chilli flakes followed by the red wine. Turn the heat to high and cook for 2–3 minutes to reduce the wine.

Turn down the heat to medium, add the mushrooms and cook for a further 5 minutes then add the tomato sauce or the chopped tomatoes and vegetable stock. Bring to the boil then reduce to a simmer, add the basil and parsley and cook on a low heat for an hour, stirring regularly.

While the ragù is cooking, make the béchamel sauce. Slowly melt the butter in a medium saucepan over a low heat. Once the butter has melted, add the flour and stir until the mixture has a paste-like consistency. Add the milk slowly, starting with one-third of the milk, whisking to form the base of the béchamel.

Add the bay leaf, nutmeg and mustard and mix well. Once the sauce starts to slightly thicken, add the remaining milk, then whisk the sauce constantly until it has thickened enough to coat the back of a wooden spoon. Once thickened, take off the heat, add the cheese and season with salt and pepper.

When the ragù sauce is ready, add the cooked lentils and stir to combine. Season with salt and pepper and take off the heat.

You can now build your lasagne. Use a 30 x 22cm rectangular roasting tin. Remove the bay leaves from the ragù and béchamel sauce. Start by spreading a small amount of the mushroom ragù evenly over the base of the roasting tin. Place a layer of lasagne sheets over the top. Spread béchamel sauce over the lasagne sheets, then a layer of the ragù. Add another layer of lasagne sheets and repeat with béchamel sauce followed by ragù.

Add one last layer of lasagne sheets, then spread the remaining béchamel sauce on top. Roughly tear the mozzarella and scatter evenly over the top of the lasagne and season with salt and pepper.

FOR THE LASAGNE
dried lasagne sheets
150g buffalo mozzarella
 (make sure it's vegetarian)

Let the lasagne rest for an hour before you put it into the oven if you have the time. It lets the sauce settle into the lasagne sheets, which enhances the texture and flavour.

Preheat the oven to 180°C Fan/200°C/Gas Mark 6. Bake the lasagne in the oven for 40 minutes until beautiful and golden on top.

Leave to cool for 20 minutes before cutting and serving. It may be hard to wait with the aroma of it all, but you will thank yourself at the table, because giving the lasagne a chance to set a little means it retains its shape without being a sloppy mess when you serve it.

Serve the lasagne with a light green salad of seasonal greens and pine nuts, simply dressed with some quality olive oil and lemon juice.

MasterChef Tip: *If you have any rinds of hard cheese in the fridge, try popping the rind into the ragù 10–15 minutes before the sauce is done to add some extra flavour.*

What makes a great tomato sauce? Great tomatoes. When they're ripe and abundant, that's the time of the year to get chopping. Buy fresh local ones instead of using canned tomatoes that may have racked up a lot of air miles to get to your cupboard. The beauty of having a fresh tomato sauce on hand is that it can be used in so many different ways, like the Mushroom & Lentil Lasagne on page 176, the Orecchiette on page 221 or the Pumpkin Gnocchi on page 172. Whatever you choose to use tomato sauce for, when you make one with fresh, local and in-season tomatoes you can really taste the difference and it's also a wonderful reminder that sunny summer days are upon you.

CLASSIC TOMATO SAUCE

MAKES ABOUT 1 LITRE

80ml extra virgin olive oil
2 brown onions, roughly chopped
3.5kg very ripe and in-season tomatoes, quartered
2 tablespoons sea salt
25g basil leaves
1–2 teaspoons caster sugar (optional)

Heat the olive oil in a large saucepan or small stockpot over a medium heat. Add the onions and cook for 5–10 minutes until they become soft but without letting them take on any colour.

Add the tomatoes and salt and cook until the tomatoes start to break down. Once they have all started to break down slightly, reduce the heat to low. Cook on a low heat for 75–80 minutes, uncovered, stirring regularly. The tomatoes will start to turn a lovely deep red colour.

After 40 minutes, add the basil leaves and taste to see how sweet the tomatoes are (this will depend on the variety and the time of year). If the sauce needs more sweetness, add 1–2 teaspoons of caster sugar to balance the flavour.

Pass the tomato sauce through a potato ricer or a fine sieve into a bowl and leave to cool. The tomato sauce will last up to 1 week, covered, in the fridge.

against
the clock

A staple for many vegetarians, protein-rich hummus combines garlic and tahini with the freshness of lemon. Chickpeas are traditional but you can use other beans, such as the butterbeans used here, for a more mellow flavour – or try adding cooked root vegetables such as beetroot or carrot. The beauty of hummus is its versatility. Serve it simply with bread at any time of day, use as a spread in a wrap or as a sauce-like component to a main meal like the Grilled Vegetables, Olives and Pitta Bread on page 52.

BUTTERBEAN HUMMUS

MAKES ROUGHLY 300G

2 garlic cloves, peeled
100ml olive oil, plus extra
    to drizzle
400g can butterbeans, drained
30ml water
2 thyme sprigs, leaves picked
½ teaspoon ground cumin
½ teaspoon smoked paprika
½ tablespoon tahini
1 tablespoon lemon juice
sea salt and freshly ground
    black pepper

Preheat the oven to 180°C Fan/200°C/Gas Mark 6.

Put the 2 garlic cloves on an oven tray, drizzle with olive oil and roast in the oven for 10 minutes until they are golden and soft.

Put all of the ingredients, except the salt and pepper, in a food processor and blend until smooth. Taste to see if the hummus needs a little more lemon juice. Season well with sea salt and pepper.

Store the hummus covered in the fridge for up to 5 days.

MasterChef Tip: *Every batch of hummus is different so taste while seasoning to get the balance right. Some days lemons will be more acidic, or you may use a different brand or type of oil, which can affect the outcome. Spread hummus and spread joy.*

It's often meat or fish that are deep-fried but these delicious little bites will knock your socks off. Cauliflower has such amazing texture and holds up so well when it's deep-fried. The whole of the cauliflower can be used. Reserve the stalk for soup, and use the leaves to make lovely crisps.

CAULIFLOWER POPCORN
WITH PEANUT OKONOMI DIPPING SAUCE

SERVES 4 AS PART OF A MEZZE-
STYLE MEAL

100ml coconut milk
1 tablespoon sriracha hot sauce
1 tablespoon soy sauce
125g plain flour
1 teaspoon sea salt
½ teaspoon freshly ground
    black pepper
½ teaspoon garlic powder
½ teaspoon onion powder
½ large head cauliflower, cut into
    bite-size pieces
sunflower oil, for deep frying

FOR THE PEANUT OKONOMI DIP
100g unsalted roasted peanuts,
    chopped
200ml okonomi sauce (a thick,
    savoury-sweet Japanese
    condiment)
1 tablespoon rice vinegar
1 tablespoon soy sauce
½ tablespoon finely grated ginger
2 teaspoons honey
1 teaspoon chilli flakes

Put the coconut milk, sriracha and soy sauce in one bowl and whisk to combine. In another bowl, stir together the flour, salt and pepper, garlic powder and onion powder. Taking a few of the cauliflower pieces at a time, dip them first into the coconut mixture, then dip them in the flour mixture.

Make sure to really work the cauliflower into the flour as it will give a lovely crunchy coating when fried. For the best results, try to let the coated cauliflower pieces sit for 10–15 minutes before frying. This will give the flour coating time to form a good crust that will not pull away as it fries.

If you have a deep-fat fryer, put the sunflower oil in it and set the temperature to 180°C. Otherwise, fill a large, heavy-based saucepan one-third full with the oil. Heat until the oil reaches 180°C when tested on a food thermometer. The oil is hot enough when a small piece of bread dropped into it floats to the top and turns golden in 20 seconds.

While the oil is heating, make the dip. Combine all the dip ingredients in a mixing bowl, then stir to combine. Set aside until it's time to serve the cauliflower.

Depending on the size of your fryer/saucepan, start to carefully lower the pieces into the hot oil. Make sure not to overcrowd the fryer/pan, or it will bring the temperature of the oil down and result in soggy cauliflower popcorn, so fry in batches as needed.

Fry the cauliflower popcorn for 3–4 minutes, remove with a slotted spoon and drain well on a plate lined with kitchen paper. Serve with the peanut okonomi dip.

MasterChef Tip: *To make cauliflower leaf crisps, toss the leaves in a little oil and sea salt and roast in the oven for 5–8 minutes at 180°C Fan/200°C/Gas Mark 6.*

Chips, glorious chips. Served with a mighty burger or eaten on their own as a snack, they are loved universally. Ordinary potato chips are amazing, but a deep-fat fryer is required. The simplicity of oven-baking makes these quick to prepare and a healthier alternative. There is a secret ingredient needed to get that crispy, bubbly exterior: cornflour. And you still keep the gloriously fluffy, sweet insides.

SWEET POTATO FRIES
WITH SRIRACHA & LIME YOGURT

SERVES 4 AS A SIDE

1½ tablespoons cornflour
1 teaspoon smoked paprika
1 teaspoon dried oregano
650g sweet potatoes, scrubbed
   and cut into 0.5–1cm fries
2 tablespoons olive oil

FOR THE SRIRACHA & LIME YOGURT
120g natural yogurt
60g soured cream
zest and juice of 1 lime
2 tablespoons sriracha hot sauce
sea salt

Preheat the oven to 200°C Fan/220°C/Gas Mark 7.

Mix together the cornflour, smoked paprika and oregano in a bowl. In a separate bowl, toss the sweet potato fries with the olive oil, then toss in the bowl with the cornflour mixture to coat well.

Spread the fries over the base of 1–2 oven trays lined with baking parchment, making sure that they are all well spaced out and in a single layer.

Bake the fries in the oven for 20 minutes, giving them a turn halfway through.

While the fries are baking, make the sriracha and lime yogurt. Combine the yogurt, soured cream, lime and sriracha in a bowl. Taste and season with a little sea salt.

Once the fries are crispy and golden on the outside and soft in the middle, remove them from the oven and let them rest for a few minutes. Season with sea salt and serve with the sriracha and lime yogurt.

Frustratingly, even a vegetarian or plant-based diet may not have the lightest carbon footprint, depending on how far the veg has travelled on its journey to the plate. The rise of smashed avocado – the opposite of eating locally – is a case in point. But we can help the environment by considering food miles, and eating as locally as possible – such as enjoying beans and peas in season. Their sweetness, with the saltiness of goat's cheese and texture of the dukkah, is a wonderful combination. The dukkah recipe makes more than enough to use in a range of other recipes so keep leftovers in a sealed jar. It's also good sprinkled over poached eggs.

SMASHED BROAD BEANS & PEAS ON SOURDOUGH
WITH GOAT'S CHEESE, DUKKAH & MINT

SERVES 2

80g shelled broad beans
80g peas
1 tablespoon olive oil, plus extra
   for brushing
1 teaspoon lemon juice
1 tablespoon finely shredded
   mint, plus extra to garnish
4 small slices sourdough
25g goat's cheese
10g dukkah (see recipe below)
sea salt and freshly ground
   black pepper

FOR THE DUKKAH

50g hazelnuts
1 tablespoon coriander seeds
½ tablespoon cumin seeds
3 tablespoons sesame seeds
½ teaspoon chilli flakes
½ teaspoon sea salt

To begin, make the dukkah. Preheat the oven to 180°C Fan/200°C/Gas Mark 6, put the hazelnuts on an oven tray and toast in the oven for 10 minutes. Heat a frying pan over a low heat and toast the coriander, cumin and sesame seeds for 1–2 minutes.

Pulse the toasted hazelnuts, seeds, chilli flakes and salt in a food processor until the mixture has a rough texture (don't let it get too fine).

Bring a saucepan of salted water to the boil and cook the broad beans and peas for 3–5 minutes. Drain in a colander and run cold water over them. Transfer to a mixing bowl and mash using a potato masher (or wear food gloves and mash with your hands). Add the olive oil, lemon juice and shredded mint and season. Set aside.

If you have a ridged grill pan, brush the sourdough slices with a little olive oil and toast in the hot pan until it has some nice char marks. Otherwise a toaster will work perfectly fine. Once the sourdough is toasted, spread the bean and pea mixture over the sourdough.

Crumble the goat's cheese over the top, then sprinkle over the dukkah. Finish with a little extra mint to garnish.

These moreish little morsels make a fantastic quick canapé, or serve them with a salad for a light lunch – this is great with the Tomato and Roast Fennel Salad on page 60. The red pepper jam will keep in the fridge for up to 2 weeks. It's great spread on sandwiches or served with cheese and biscuits.

COURGETTE, PEA & HALLOUMI CAKES
WITH RED PEPPER CHILLI JAM

MAKES ABOUT 16

2 courgettes (500g), grated
150g frozen peas, defrosted
220g halloumi, grated
2 tablespoons chopped coriander
1 tablespoon chopped dill
200g plain flour
2 teaspoons baking powder
100ml olive oil
sea salt and freshly ground
    black pepper

FOR THE RED PEPPER CHILLI JAM
2 tablespoons olive oil
3 red chillies, chopped
    (2 deseeded, 1 with seeds)
2 garlic cloves, finely chopped
4 red peppers, deseeded and
    roughly chopped
400g can chopped tomatoes
2 tablespoons rice vinegar
100g caster sugar

Preheat the oven to 180°C Fan/200°C/Gas Mark 6.

Begin by making the red pepper chilli jam. Heat the olive oil in a saucepan over a medium heat and cook the chillies, garlic and red peppers, stirring, for 2–3 minutes. Add the tomatoes, vinegar and sugar and bring to the boil.

Reduce the heat to low, then simmer for an hour, making sure to stir regularly until the jam becomes quite thick. Let the jam cool in the saucepan to set and thicken up further.

Put the grated courgette in a clean piece of muslin or a clean tea towel inside a colander, then hang the colander over a bowl. Give the courgettes a pinch of salt. Tie the muslin/towel and squeeze as hard as you can to get as much moisture as you can from the courgette. Repeat this process a few times until the courgette is quite dry.

For the cakes, combine the courgette, peas, halloumi, coriander, dill, flour and baking powder in a mixing bowl. Combine well and season with a good amount of pepper but just a little salt as the halloumi is quite salty.

Heat the olive oil in a frying pan and fry the cakes in batches. Use a heaped dessertspoon per cake and shape with your hands to form a fritter shape. Cook for 2 minutes on each side until crisp and golden. Remove with a slotted spoon and drain on kitchen paper. When all the cakes are cooked, transfer them to an oven tray lined with baking parchment and heat in the oven for 10 minutes or until warmed through. Serve with the red pepper chilli jam.

MasterChef Tip: *The jam will make more than required but is great served with Lentil & Mushroom Sausage Rolls on page 109.*

The sandwich is the classic British quick-fix lunch. Its predecessor, the open sandwich, hails from the Middle Ages when slabs of bread were used as plates, slathered with butter and the fillings heaped on top. This Scandinavian-inspired open sandwich is ideal for those long, sunny al fresco lunches, or as a fresh yet filling brunch.

ASPARAGUS, EGG & POTATO OPEN SANDWICHES
WITH SEAWEED MAYO

SERVES 2

2 eggs
160g new potatoes, quartered
6 asparagus spears, cut into
   2cm pieces
4 slices sourdough
extra virgin olive oil to brush
2 radishes, finely sliced
dill sprigs, to garnish
sea salt flakes and freshly ground
   black pepper

FOR THE SEAWEED MAYO
60g mayonnaise
30g crème fraîche
½ tablespoon lemon juice
½ tablespoon dulse (dried red
   seaweed) flakes or nori,
   finely chopped

Bring a saucepan of water to the boil, carefully lower in the eggs and cook for 6½ minutes. Remove from the pan, then run the eggs under cold water. When cool enough to handle, carefully peel the eggs and set aside.

Meanwhile, in another saucepan, blanch the potatoes in boiling water for 7–8 minutes until tender when tested with the tip of a sharp knife, then drain and leave to cool. Use the same pan to blanch the asparagus in boiling water for 30 seconds to 1 minute, then plunge into cold water and drain.

For the seaweed mayo, combine the mayonnaise, crème fraîche, lemon juice and dulse in a bowl and season with salt and pepper.

Heat a ridged grill pan over a high heat and brush the sourdough slices with extra virgin olive oil. Toast in the pan until the bread has some nice char marks.

To build the sandwiches, start by spreading some of the seaweed mayo over each piece of toasted sourdough, then layer over the potato, asparagus and radishes. Top each piece with half a boiled egg and dill sprigs, and season with sea salt flakes and pepper. Serve with extra seaweed mayo on the side.

This recipe is inspired by the Hakka-style stuffed tofu that I always loved as a child. Umami-packed, with a crispy skin and fiery flavours, this is a perfect meal even when you're against the clock. Tofu is a great source of plant protein and pairs easily with many flavours. To transform such a simple ingredient into a show-stopping delicacy, first I stuff the tofu with shiitake mushrooms then add a crispy texture by frying it with chillies and garlic – you don't need to sacrifice *MasterChef* quality food just because you're short of time!

CRISPY TOFU PARCELS
WITH SHIITAKE MUSHROOMS

SERVES 2

500g firm tofu
cornflour, for dusting

FOR THE FILLING
1 tablespoon vegetable oil
125g shiitake mushrooms,
**   finely chopped**
1 tablespoon vegan oyster sauce
freshly ground black pepper

TO FINISH
vegetable oil, for frying
1 tablespoon finely chopped
**   garlic**
1 red chilli, finely sliced (deseed if
**   you prefer less heat)**
2 spring onions, finely sliced,
**   white and green parts**
**   separated**
1 tablespoon five-spice powder
1 teaspoon ground white pepper
pinch of sea salt

Preheat the oven to 180°C Fan/200°C/Gas Mark 6.

For the tofu parcels, pat the tofu dry using kitchen paper. Cut the tofu into 6cm squares. For each square, hollow out a 2cm square to form a cavity. Alternatively, scoop out about 1 teaspoon of tofu from each piece to make room for the filling. (The excess tofu can be used in another recipe, such as stir-fry or soup.)

For the filling, heat a frying pan over a medium heat and, when hot, add the oil. Add the shiitake mushrooms and fry, stirring, until they're softened, about 5 minutes. Add the vegan oyster sauce, give it a good mix and season with freshly ground black pepper.

Stuff the cavity of each tofu parcel with the cooked shiitakes. Lightly dust the stuffed tofu parcels with cornflour.

Transfer the parcels to a lined baking tray, then bake for 10–15 minutes, or until the surface is brown and crispy.

To finish, heat 1 tablespoon of vegetable oil in a pan over a medium-high heat. When hot, add the garlic, chilli and the white part of the spring onions. Cook for 1 minute, stirring, then add the five-spice powder and ground white pepper. Give it a good stir then cook for 1 minute. Add salt to taste.

To serve, top the tofu parcels with the garlic and chillies and garnish with the green part of the spring onions. Perfect with rice and stir-fried vegetables.

One-tray wonders are a blessing during the busy working week. Dishes that require just chopping a few vegetables and adding a few other ingredients, then a half-hour unattended in the oven are perfect. The deep savoury-sweet combination of miso with a sriracha kick really works a treat. Add some steamed rice to make it a main dish, and a satisfyingly simple dinner is served.

MISO & SRIRACHA GLAZED VEGETABLE TRAY BAKE

SERVES 2 AS A MAIN OR 4 AS A SIDE

1 aubergine, cut into large pieces
250g chestnut mushrooms,
   cut into thirds
2 tablespoons olive oil
100g tenderstem broccoli,
   cut in half

FOR THE MISO & SRIRACHA GLAZE
2 tablespoons miso paste
2 tablespoons soy sauce
2 tablespoons rice vinegar
1 tablespoon water
1 tablespoon sriracha hot sauce
2 teaspoons honey

TO SERVE
toasted sesame seeds
1 spring onion, cut into rounds
½ red chilli, cut into rounds
steamed rice, if having as a main

Preheat the oven to 200°C Fan/220°C/Gas Mark 7.

Toss the aubergine and mushrooms with the olive oil in a mixing bowl, spread over the base of a roasting tray and roast for 20 minutes.

While the aubergine and mushrooms are roasting, in another mixing bowl mix together all of the glaze ingredients and set aside.

Once the aubergine and mushrooms have had 20 minutes in the oven, remove from the oven, pour over the glaze, then mix together to coat the vegetables thoroughly in the sauce. Return to the oven for a further 15 minutes.

When there is 5 minutes' cooking time remaining for the aubergine and mushrooms, add the tenderstem broccoli to the roasting tray and return to the oven for 5 minutes.

Garnish with the sesame seeds, spring onions and red chilli. Serve as a side dish or as a main with steamed rice.

This is a great midweek one-tray wonder that does all of the work for itself, leaving you time to unwind a little or get on with other tasks. The sweetness of the cherry tomatoes combined with a tad of saffron, paired with the texture and crunch of the almonds and sesame seeds, really makes this bake sing.

PEARL BARLEY & CAULIFLOWER BAKE

SERVES 2–3

200g pearl barley
4 shallots, sliced
1 garlic clove, finely chopped
1 teaspoon thyme leaves
600ml vegetable stock
12 cherry tomatoes, halved
pinch of saffron threads
400g cauliflower, cut into florets
  and leaves reserved
olive oil, for drizzling
20g watercress
½ tablespoon almonds, toasted
  in a dry pan
½ tablespoon sesame seeds,
  toasted in a dry pan
sea salt and freshly ground
  black pepper

Preheat the oven to 180°C Fan/200°C/Gas Mark 6.

Put the pearl barley, shallots, garlic and thyme in a roasting tin, pour over the vegetable stock, then add the cherry tomatoes and saffron. Season with salt and pepper and stir well to combine.

Cover the roasting tin with foil and bake for 25 minutes. After 25 minutes remove the foil and add the cauliflower florets and cauliflower leaves. Give the florets and leaves a small drizzle of olive oil and roast for another 20 minutes uncovered. Leave the bake to rest for 5 minutes before serving.

Top with the watercress and sprinkle the almonds and sesame seeds over the bake. Serve with steamed green vegetables or Little Gem, Pea & Quinoa Salad (see page 71).

MasterChef Tip: *To avoid wasting any part of the vegetable, always use the cauliflower leaves. Roasted, they become delicious crisps.*

Served as a main or as a side, this dish is sure to impress. Roasting broccoli brings out its array of flavours and textures. The stalk has a lovely nutty taste while the florets are crisp, slightly charred and beautifully caramelised. Sherry vinegar and currants give the broccoli the ideal amount of tartness and sweetness. As an added bonus, this dish is super-quick and simple to prepare. If you are looking for an alternative to nut roast for Sunday lunch, this is will be a hit.

ROAST BROCCOLI
WITH GARLIC, SHERRY VINEGAR & HAZELNUTS

SERVES 2 AS A MAIN OR 4 AS A SIDE

2 garlic cloves, finely sliced
½ red chilli, roughly chopped
2 tablespoons sherry vinegar
4 tablespoons olive oil
zest of ½ lemon
1 large head of broccoli, halved
2 tablespoons hazelnuts, toasted
** in a dry pan and chopped**
2 tablespoons currants
handful flat-leaf parsley,
** finely chopped**
good pinch of sea salt

Preheat the oven to 180°C Fan/200°C/Gas Mark 6.

In a mixing bowl, combine the garlic, chilli, sherry vinegar, olive oil and lemon zest and season with salt. Add the broccoli halves to the bowl with the marinade and massage well into the broccoli.

Transfer the broccoli to a roasting tin, drizzle over the marinade from the mixing bowl, then roast in the oven for 20 minutes. The broccoli should be slightly charred in parts while still retaining some firmness and bite to it.

Serve the broccoli with the hazelnuts, currants and parsley sprinkled over the top. If you're having the broccoli as a main, try serving it with the Artichoke, Orange & Pearl Barley Salad (see page 53).

This Japanese classic is loved by so many and its intense, fragrant flavours reveal why – the subtle spices, the kick of heat and the little bit of sweetness make a wonderful combination. The chicken may no longer be on the plate but it's the union of the curry sauce and super-crispy panko coating that makes katsu curry so memorable. Try serving with Miso & Sriracha Glazed Vegetable Tray Bake (see page 200) alongside some steamed rice.

SWEET POTATO KATSU CURRY

SERVES 4

2 tablespoons sunflower oil
1 brown onion, finely sliced
1 tablespoon finely grated ginger
2 garlic cloves, finely chopped
1½ tablespoons madras
curry powder
1 teaspoon chilli flakes
3 tablespoons plain flour
750ml vegetable stock, hot
60ml soy sauce
1 tablespoon honey
1 tablespoon rice vinegar

FOR THE CRUMBED SWEET POTATO
2 eggs, lightly beaten
40g plain flour
200g panko breadcrumbs
500g sweet potatoes, scrubbed
and cut into 0.5cm slices
100ml sunflower oil, for shallow
frying

TO SERVE
4 tablespoons crispy fried
shallots
6g coriander leaves
steamed rice

Begin by making the curry sauce. Heat the 2 tablespoons of sunflower oil in a saucepan over a low to medium heat, add the onions and cook, stirring, for 5 minutes until they are starting to become soft. Add the ginger and garlic and cook for 1–2 minutes.

Add the curry powder and chilli flakes and cook for a further minute to release their aromas. Add the flour and mix to form a paste with the onion mixture, then add the vegetable stock in stages, stirring constantly between additions.

Bring to the boil then reduce the heat and simmer the curry sauce for 15 minutes until the sauce has thickened. Add the soy sauce, honey and rice vinegar, let it simmer for a further 5 minutes, then taste to check the seasoning and add a little salt if needed. Remove from the heat.

Preheat the oven to 180°C Fan/200°C/Gas Mark 6.

To crumb the sweet potato, put the beaten eggs, flour and panko in 3 separate shallow bowls. Taking one piece of sweet potato at a time, dip it in the flour first, followed by the egg and finally the breadcrumbs. Repeat the process with all of the sweet potato slices.

Heat the 100ml of sunflower oil in a large frying pan over a medium heat. Working in batches, shallow fry the crumbed sweet potato slices until golden on each side, for roughly 3 minutes per side. Transfer the cooked slices to an oven tray. When all slices are breadcrumbed, transfer the tray to the oven and cook for a further 10–12 minutes until the sweet potato is tender when tested with the tip of a sharp knife.

Put the cooked sweet potato on plates or in shallow bowls and ladle over the katsu sauce. Garnish with the crispy fried shallots and coriander and serve with steamed rice.

Plums and tomatoes are two great-tasting fruits that can be combined at their seasonal peak in late summer and autumn. This is a fresh, quick salad, with added protein from tofu and a little chilli spice.

PLUM & TOMATO SALAD
WITH CRISPY TOFU & CHILLI SALT

SERVES 4

2–3 tablespoons olive oil
400g firm tofu, cut into
   2cm cubes
cornflour, for dusting
6 plums, stoned and quartered
6 large ripe tomatoes, cut into
   chunks
30g rocket
6g basil leaves, torn

FOR THE CHILLI SALT
4 tablespoons sea salt flakes
4 teaspoons chilli flakes

FOR THE DRESSING
60ml extra virgin olive oil
1½ tablespoons balsamic vinegar
pinch of sea salt

To make the chilli salt, put the salt and chilli flakes in a mortar and pestle and roughly grind. This will make more than needed but it makes for a great seasoning with other dishes. Just keep the leftovers in a sealed jar.

Whisk the dressing ingredients in a small bowl and set aside.

Heat the olive oil in a frying pan over a medium to high heat. Dust the tofu cubes with the cornflour then fry the cubes for a minute on each side. Drain on kitchen paper, season well with the chilli salt and set aside.

In a mixing bowl, combine the plums, tomatoes, rocket and basil, then dress with the dressing. Serve the salad in bowls and top with the crispy tofu for a lovely light summer lunch.

See pages 208–209 for the recipe photograph.

Omelettes are the ultimate whip-up-quick meal. All you need are some eggs, some vegetables, maybe some cheese and you have a meal ready in a matter of minutes. Kimchi and eggs are the perfect pairing and this omelette is an explosion of flavours and textures. The lovely balance of spicy, salty and sweet, the softness of the eggs and the crunch of the kimchi are delightful.

KIMCHI & BEANSPROUT OMELETTE
WITH THAI BASIL

SERVES 1

1 tablespoon sunflower oil
3 eggs, whisked
1 teaspoon light soy sauce
2 spring onions, finely sliced
50g Kimchi (see page 63),
    roughly chopped
30g beansprouts
small handful each of Thai basil
    and coriander
pinch of ground pepper

TO SERVE
sriracha hot sauce
soy sauce
lime wedges

Heat the oil in a wok or frying pan over a medium to high heat. Whisk the eggs in a bowl then add the soy sauce and spring onions and season with pepper.

Pour the egg mixture into the hot wok/frying pan and, working in a circular motion, tilt the wok/frying pan from side to side so the egg mixture starts to settle up the sides. Cook for 1 minute then add the kimchi and beansprouts. Continue cooking the omelette for a further 2 minutes, moving the omelette around a little in the wok/frying pan but not scrambling it.

Take the wok/frying pan off the heat, add the Thai basil and coriander, then fold the omelette in half and use a spatula to carefully transfer to a serving plate.

See pages 212–213 for the recipe photograph.

For speed combined with healthy deliciousness, it's hard to beat a good stir-fry. Skill and speed are required, so preparation is crucial. Have all of your ingredients prepped and ready, close by to your already-hot wok. The Szechuan pepper takes this dish to a new level with its strong and hot flavour. If you can, grind whole Szechuan peppercorns and the taste will be insanely aromatic.

TOFU & SHIITAKE SZECHUAN STIR-FRY
WITH PEANUTS

SERVES 2 AS A MAIN OR 4 AS A SIDE

3 tablespoons sunflower oil
3 spring onions, cut into 2–3cm
   lengths
2 garlic cloves, finely sliced
2cm piece ginger, peeled and cut
   into thin strips
½ teaspoon ground Szechuan
   peppercorns
200g shiitake mushrooms, torn
1 pak choy, roughly chopped
1 tablespoon soy sauce
½ tablespoon rice vinegar
1–2 tablespoons cornflour

FOR THE TOFU
1 tablespoon soy sauce
½ tablespoon rice vinegar
1 teaspoon toasted sesame oil
200g firm tofu, cut into
   1–2cm cubes

TO SERVE
steamed rice
1 tablespoon unsalted peanuts,
   toasted and chopped

Begin by marinating the tofu. Combine the soy sauce, vinegar and sesame oil in a bowl, add the tofu cubes and toss to combine. Leave the tofu to marinate for 15–20 minutes.

Heat 1½ tablespoons of the sunflower oil in a wok or frying pan over a high heat and cook the spring onions for 1–2 minutes. Add the garlic, ginger and Szechuan pepper and toss to combine. Add the mushrooms and pak choy along with the soy sauce and vinegar and cook for another 1–2 minutes. Remove from the wok/pan and set aside (keep the wok/pan to hand).

Dust the marinated tofu in the cornflour. Heat the remaining sunflower oil in the wok/pan over a high heat. Add the tofu and cook, stirring, for 2–3 minutes, making sure to cook on all sides so the cubes are lovely and crispy and golden. Add the mushrooms and pak choy back to the wok/pan along with a splash of water and heat through, stirring.

Serve with steamed rice, and with the toasted peanuts scattered over the top.

What I love about a Sri Lankan curry is how quickly you can serve up an intricately layered and fragrant meal. Small green chillies will provide a little more heat than your usual red ones, and the fresh coconut and mint sambol served on the side brings the dish to life one little spoonful at a time.

SRI LANKAN LENTIL & POTATO CURRY
WITH MINT SAMBOL

SERVES 4

2 tablespoons sunflower oil
5 shallots, finely chopped
3 garlic cloves, finely chopped
3cm piece ginger, grated
3–4 small green chillies,
**   finely chopped**
1 tablespoon curry powder
½ tablespoon black
**   mustard seeds**
1 teaspoon ground fenugreek
1 teaspoon ground turmeric
½ teaspoon ground cinnamon
2 large tomatoes, chopped
500g Maris Piper potatoes,
**   cut into 2cm pieces**
400ml can coconut milk
200ml water
400g can lentils, drained
150g baby spinach
juice of ½ lime

FOR THE MINT SAMBOL
50g unsweetened desiccated
**   coconut**
12g mint leaves, chopped
5g coriander, chopped
1 garlic clove, finely chopped
¼ red onion, finely chopped
½ tablespoon lime juice, plus
**   1 teaspoon zest**
pinch of sea salt

TO SERVE
chopped coriander
steamed rice and/or roti
**   or naan bread**

Heat the sunflower oil in a saucepan over a medium heat. Add the shallots, garlic, ginger and chillies and cook, stirring, for 2–3 minutes until soft. Add the curry powder, mustard seeds, fenugreek, turmeric and cinnamon and cook for a further minute.

Add the tomatoes and potatoes and stir to coat with the spice mix. Add the coconut milk and water and bring to the boil. Reduce the heat to medium-low and cook the curry for 15 minutes, stirring occasionally.

While the curry is cooking, make the mint sambol. Combine all the ingredients in a bowl, mix well and set aside.

After 15 minutes, use the tip of a sharp knife to test the potatoes in the curry. They should be tender and cooked through. Add the lentils and spinach and cook for a further 2–3 minutes. Season with lime juice and a little salt.

Serve the curry with the fresh mint sambol, steamed rice and/or some warmed roti or naan bread. A nice cold beer always goes down a treat with a curry too.

DINO ANGELO LUCIANO MASTERCHEF US CHAMPION 2017

Béchamel, considered one of the mother sauces of French cuisine since the seventeenth century, originated and gained its popularity between France and Italy. It's a favourite of mine since childhood; my nonna would make this dish to cheer me up, typically with its original ingredients of milk, butter, flour and whole wheat semolina pasta. Since choosing to be primarily plant-based, I needed to recreate this sauce without the butter and milk. This version is just as delicious. I decided to create it with my favourite rice noodles, thus making it gluten free as well.

This dish is succulent and full-flavoured, and tremendously healthy. The anti-inflammatory garlic, which gives this dish a smoky decadence, is a good source of vitamin C, manganese and B6, while nutritional yeast is high in B vitamins. Quick and simple, this dish is a very beautiful thing.

RICE NOODLE FETTUCCINE
WITH MUSHROOMS & BABYDOLL BÉCHAMEL

SERVES 3 AS A MAIN OR 6 AS A SIDE

200g rice noodles
225g mushrooms, quartered
   (a mix of shiitake, chanterelle
   and baby bella)
1 tablespoon olive oil
½ yellow onion, finely sliced
3 garlic cloves, finely chopped
400ml can coconut milk
2–3 tablespoons nutritional yeast
1½ teaspoons sea salt (add little
   by little and taste as you go)

TO SERVE

extra virgin olive oil
½ teaspoon black pepper
1 teaspoon fresh chopped dill
½ teaspoon red chilli flakes
   (optional)
1 lemon, sliced, for garnish
   (optional, for a fresh citrus
   summer vibe)

Get a large pan of water boiling for the rice noodles. When the water starts to boil, add a generous amount of salt. Add the noodles and cook for 2 minutes, then drain and set aside.

Heat a saucepan over a high heat, then add the mushrooms to the dry pan (with no oil) and cook, stirring, until the mushrooms start to sear, about 4–5 minutes.

Remove the mushrooms from the pan and set aside on a plate. Turn down the heat to medium, add the olive oil to the pan, then add the onion and garlic and cook, stirring. As soon as the garlic starts to brown, add the coconut milk and stir gently.

Continue cooking until the coconut milk starts to bubble, then immediately add the nutritional yeast and begin salting to taste. I've discovered that, with this amount of coconut milk, it takes precisely 1½ tablespoons to season to perfection, but add according to your taste.

Add the cooked mushrooms and cooked rice noodles to the béchamel sauce and cook on high for 1 minute, stirring constantly.

Serve on plates, drizzled with extra virgin olive oil, sprinkled with black pepper, dill and chilli flakes. Add lemon slices if you like.

Pasta often tops the list of go-to dishes to get a meal on the table, pronto. But speed doesn't have to compromise quality, and quality doesn't mean it has to be complicated. Just a few well-chosen ingredients, like orecchiette (ear-shaped pasta) instead of penne, with fresh produce can lift a meal and add vibrancy to a tired midweek rotation.

ORECCHIETTE
WITH BROCCOLI CRUMBS, LEMON & CHILLI

SERVES 4

400g orecchiette
1 small broccoli (florets and stalk), cut into chunks
1 large slice sourdough, torn into pieces
3 tablespoons olive oil
1 garlic clove, sliced
1 red chilli, deseeded and finely chopped
200ml Classic Tomato Sauce (see page 180) or 150g canned chopped tomatoes
zest of ½ lemon
sea salt and freshly ground black pepper

TO SERVE

50g vegetarian grating cheese, grated
small handful flat-leaf parsley, finely sliced

Bring a large pan of salted water to the boil and cook the orecchiette according to the packet instructions. Drain the pasta and reserve a little of the pasta water.

In a food processor, blend the broccoli and the sourdough until the mixture resembles rough breadcrumbs.

Heat the olive oil in a large frying pan over a medium heat then add the sliced garlic. Once the garlic starts to turn golden, remove the garlic using a slotted spoon and discard. Add the chilli and cook for 1 minute. Turn up the heat to high, add the broccoli and sourdough crumbs and cook, stirring, for 2–3 minutes until they start to colour.

Add the drained orecchiette along with a few tablespoons of the reserved pasta water to the pan and toss to combine. Add the tomato sauce and lemon zest and cook, stirring gently, until all is heated through. Season with fresh cracked pepper and some salt if needed and serve with grated cheese and parsley to garnish.

Fried rice may be the ultimate leftovers dish. The possibilities really are endless, depending on what you have to use up in the fridge. The addition of kimchi gives a real depth of flavour to fried rice, and is good for gut health. Be sure to use any leftover cooked rice within 24 hours, and ensure it is steaming hot throughout. Never re-heat cooked rice more than once; if it has been reheated once, discard any leftovers.

CAULIFLOWER, CORN & KIMCHI FRIED RICE

SERVES 2

2½ tablespoons sunflower oil
500g day-old steamed rice
2 eggs
20g ginger, finely grated
2 garlic cloves, finely chopped
4 spring onions, sliced
    into rounds
160g cauliflower, cut into
    small florets
60g sweetcorn, fresh or canned
150g vegetarian kimchi
1 tablespoon soy sauce
2 tablespoons chopped coriander
sriracha hot sauce, to serve
sea salt and freshly ground
    black pepper

Heat 1 tablespoon of the sunflower oil in a large wok or frying pan over a high heat then add the rice. Toss the rice until it is slightly crisp and lightly coloured, 2–3 minutes. Remove the rice from the wok/frying pan and set aside. Keep the wok/frying pan to hand.

In a separate frying pan, heat ½ tablespoon of the remaining sunflower oil and fry the eggs. Let the bottom of each egg get a little crispiness to it but not too much. Leave the yolk runny and season with salt and pepper. Set aside in the pan to keep warm.

Put the wok/frying pan back over a medium to high heat with the remaining sunflower oil, add the remaining ingredients except the coriander then toss the contents of the wok/frying pan constantly for 1–2 minutes. Add the reserved fried rice and the coriander and toss for a further minute.

Serve the fried rice with a fried egg and a drizzle of sriracha sauce over the top.

MasterChef Tip: *If you want to make fried rice but don't have any day-old rice, you can cook some fresh rice and dry it in the oven to give it the same texture. While the rice is cooking, heat the oven to 140°C Fan/160°C/Gas Mark 3. Once the rice is cooked, spread it out in a single flat layer on an oven tray and transfer to the oven to dry out a little for 15 minutes.*

Wonderfully comforting, with a layering of spices, dhal should be on the weekly rotation of quick vegetarian meals. Apart from a small amount of chopping, it's just a case of giving it a regular stir as it cooks and you're ready to serve. Traditionally, dhal is made with water or stock but the addition of coconut milk adds a lovely creamy freshness. Serve with steamed rice or, to cut the cooking time, some warm naan or roti bread.

COCONUT & CAULIFLOWER DHAL
WITH FRIED CURRY LEAVES

SERVES 6

4 tablespoons sunflower oil
10 curry leaves
1 large red onion, sliced
2 garlic cloves, finely chopped
1 tablespoon grated ginger
2 teaspoons curry powder
1 teaspoon ground cumin
½ teaspoon ground fenugreek
½ teaspoon ground turmeric
½ teaspoon chilli flakes
½ teaspoon black mustard seeds
400g brown lentils, rinsed
2 large ripe tomatoes, chopped
2 x 400ml cans coconut milk
800ml water
350g cauliflower florets, cut into
**   1cm pieces**

TO SERVE
chopped coriander, to garnish
steamed rice

First prepare the curry leaves. Heat 2 tablespoons of the oil in a frying pan over a high heat then fry the curry leaves for 2 minutes. Remove using a slotted spoon and drain on kitchen paper.

Heat the remaining 2 tablespoons of the oil in a large saucepan over a medium heat, add the onion, garlic and ginger and cook, stirring, for 2–3 minutes. Add the curry powder, cumin, fenugreek, turmeric, chilli flakes and mustard seeds and cook for another 30 seconds, stirring to release the aromas.

Add the lentils and stir to coat with the spices. Add the tomatoes, coconut milk and water. Bring to the boil then reduce to a simmer. Add the fried curry leaves and cook uncovered for 45–50 minutes, stirring regularly to prevent the dhal catching on the bottom of the pan. If the dhal gets too dry, add a little more water.

When the lentils are tender, add the cauliflower florets and cook for another 2–3 minutes.

Serve the dhal garnished with chopped coriander, and with steamed rice on the side. Dhal is wonderful with an accompaniment or two, such as a little chutney or a fiery pickle.

The earthiness of the lentils pairs so well with the lovely sweetness of roasted butternut squash, and the Stilton adds a salty richness. Don't be put off by peeling the butternut. If you're really pushed for time simply roast it with the skin on – the skin is perfectly edible and softens when roasted.

WARM SALAD OF ROASTED SQUASH, PUY LENTILS & BLUE STILTON

SERVES 4

800g butternut squash, peeled
    and cut into 2.5cm cubes
1½ tablespoons olive oil
150g cooked puy lentils
50g rocket
handful flat-leaf parsley, roughly
    chopped
160g Stilton (check that it's
    vegetarian)
good crusty bread, to serve
sea salt and freshly ground
    black pepper

FOR THE DRESSING
3 tablespoons extra virgin
    olive oil
1 tablespoon lemon juice
1 tablespoon white wine vinegar
½ tablespoon honey

Preheat the oven to 180°C Fan/200°C/Gas Mark 6.

Spread the butternut cubes over the base of a baking tray lined with baking parchment, drizzle over the olive oil, season with salt and pepper and mix well. Roast for 25–30 minutes then set aside to rest for 5 minutes.

To make the dressing, whisk together the extra virgin olive oil, lemon juice, vinegar and honey in a bowl and season with salt and pepper.

In another large bowl, combine the warm butternut, puy lentils, rocket and parsley. Add the dressing and gently mix to combine.

Serve the salad with the cheese crumbled over the top, with some good crusty bread.

MasterChef Tip: *To peel a butternut, the most time-efficient way is to use a large cook's knife. Chop it in half horizontally so that you have separated the bulbous part from the neck. Place each piece cut-side down on the chopping board. Then use the sharp knife to cut the skin off from top to bottom. Note that this is a cutting motion as opposed to a smooth peeling motion.*

index

A

almonds
crumb with green mac 'n' cheese 31
soy 163

apples
celeriac & potato salad 59
chilli coleslaw 151
spiced chutney 117
Artichoke, Orange & Pearl Barley Salad 53
Asian Coleslaw with Coconut & Lemongrass Dressing 72

asparagus
egg & potato open sandwiches with seaweed mayo 194
with fried polenta & béchamel 64
miso & seaweed broth with noodles 85

aubergine
purée with bubble & squeak 152
roasted with mushrooms & nuoc cham 132
schnitzel with fennel & chilli coleslaw 128

B

basil goat's cheese croquettes with honey & vinegar dip 103; *see also* Thai basil

beans smoky baked with wild mushrooms 99; *see also* broad beans; butterbeans

beansprouts and Kimchi omelette with Thai basil 211

béchamel sauce
asparagus & fried polenta 64
mushroom & lentil lasagne 176
rice noodle fettuccine with mushrooms 218

beetroot
glazed in soy with crisped leaves, pickled stem salad & creamy polenta 164

and grape salad with blue cheese dressing, hazelnuts & sesame seeds 75
and wheatberry salad 89

blue cheese
dressing 75
Stilton, squash & puy lentils warm salad 226
Braised Cabbage & Kale with Ricotta Polenta 159

bread
asparagus, egg & potato open sandwiches 194
courgette, smoked Cheddar & jalapeño 14
mushroom toasts with black vinegar dip 96
pangrattato 35
smashed broad beans & peas on sourdough 190

broad beans and peas smashed on sourdough with goat's cheese, dukkah & mint 190

broccoli
charred tenderstem & puy lentil salad 35
crumbs with orecchiette, lemon & chilli 221
roast with garlic, sherry vinegar & hazelnuts 204
sauce with courgette 'spaghetti' 25

broths
miso, asparagus & seaweed with noodles 85
pearl barley, cavolo nero & saffron mayo 18

Brussels sprouts
and hispi cabbage laksa 171
salad with quick-pickled cabbage, capers & nigella seeds 76
Bubble & Squeak with Roast Aubergine Purée, Herbed Yogurt & Quick-Pickled Shallots 152
Buddha Bowls with Tahini Green Goddess Dressing & Soy Almonds 163

bulgur wheat
roast carrots & lentil salad 80
squash koftas with tomato sauce & pine nuts 81

burgers
corn fritter with mango salsa & gochujang mayo 118
'quarter pounder' 44

butterbeans
hummus 52, 185
hummus with padrón peppers 68
hummus with roasted radishes & quinoa 67

butternut squash
and bulgur wheat koftas with tomato sauce 81
gnocchi with sage, tomato & pumpkin crisps 172
puy lentils & blue Stilton warm salad 226
soup with turmeric, lemongrass & cashew salsa 86

butters
jalapeño 104
miso 127

C

cabbage
braised with kale & ricotta polenta 159
bubble & squeak with aubergine purée, herbed yogurt & pickled shallots 152
charred hispi with miso butter & togarashi 127
hispi and Brussels sprout laksa 171
see also coleslaw; red cabbage

capers
Brussels sprout salad 76
tomato & roast fennel salad 60

caponata with polenta & griddled gem lettuce 26

carrots lentil & bulgur wheat salad 80

cashew nuts salsa 86

cauliflower
and coconut dhal with fried curry leaves 225
corn & Kimchi fried rice 222
and pearl barley bake 203
popcorn with peanut okonomi dipping sauce 186

CONVERSION TABLES

WEIGHTS

METRIC	IMPERIAL
15g	½oz
20g	¾oz
30g	1oz
55g	2oz
85g	3oz
110g	4oz / ¼lb
140g	5oz
170g	6oz
200g	7oz
225g	8oz / ½lb
255g	9oz
285g	10oz
310g	11oz
340g	12oz / ¾lb
370g	13oz
400g	14oz
425g	15oz
450g	16oz / 1lb
1kg	2lb 4oz
1.5kg	3lb 5oz

LIQUIDS

METRIC	IMPERIAL
5ml	1 teaspoon
15ml	1 tablespoon or ½fl oz
30ml	2 tablespoons or 1fl oz
150ml	¼ pint or 5fl oz
290ml	½ pint or 10fl oz
425ml	¾ pint or 16fl oz
570ml	1 pint or 20fl oz
1 litre	1¾ pints
1.2 litres	2 pints

LENGTH

METRIC	IMPERIAL
5mm	¼in
1cm	½in
2cm	¾in
2.5cm	1in
5cm	2in
10cm	4in
15cm	6in
20cm	8in
30cm	12in

USEFUL CONVERSIONS

1 tablespoon	= 3 teaspoons
1 level tablespoon	= approx. 15g or ½oz
1 heaped tablespoon	= approx. 30g or 1oz
1 egg	= 55ml / 55g / 1fl oz

OVEN TEMPERATURES

°C	°C FAN	GAS MARK	°F
110°C	90°C Fan	Gas Mark ¼	225°F
120°C	100°C Fan	Gas Mark ½	250°F
140°C	120°C Fan	Gas Mark 1	275°F
150°C	130°C Fan	Gas Mark 2	300°F
160°C	140°C Fan	Gas Mark 3	325°F
180°C	160°C Fan	Gas Mark 4	350°F
190°C	170°C Fan	Gas Mark 5	375°F
200°C	180°C Fan	Gas Mark 6	400°F
220°C	200°C Fan	Gas Mark 7	425°F
230°C	210°C Fan	Gas Mark 8	450°F
240°C	220°C Fan	Gas Mark 9	475°F

ACKNOWLEDGEMENTS

I would like to thank a few people for all of their support and guidance in writing my first cookbook, *MasterChef Green*. It has been a wonderful ride, and literally a dream come true for me; when I started out as a chef some twenty years ago, my first dream was not to open my own restaurant but to write a book. Well, here is that dream in reality.

It has been an amazing experience to be given the opportunity to promote a more vegetable-led way of eating. To bring healthy eating, sustainability and great cooking into one book has been inspiring. Writing *MasterChef Green* has helped to shape me both professionally and personally, and that is something that I am very grateful for.

As excited as I am for people to start cooking the recipes in this book, they would not have been laid to page without the help of the following superstars.

Firstly, to everyone at Absolute. My biggest of thanks from the bottom of my heart for making a dream come true. To the legend that is Jon Croft, thank you for giving this unknown a shot and making it happen. To Emily North, I would have been lost through this process without you and all of your constant support and guidance. And to the wonderful design team of Pete Moffat and Anika Schulze – thank you.

I would also like to thank the team at Endemol Shine Group for their support and for letting me showcase vegetarian cooking the *MasterChef* way. While talking about *MasterChef*, I cannot forget to thank the amazing contestants for their incredible recipe contributions.

It is often family who are the ones supporting us as we try to achieve our goals. This is true in my case, and even more so during a worldwide pandemic, so many thank yous are due. Firstly, to my Mum, Debs, and sisters Kristy and Lisa: thanks for the support from day one of my food journey, and for being understanding every time I've missed things due to work. To my in-laws, Mus and Paul, a massive thanks for babysitting during the photoshoot, and to my brother-in-law Jamie for your guidance and expert help in all things photography-based.

Lastly, to my beautiful wife, art director, co-photographer and prop stylist, Marie O'Shepherd. You are the one who has helped and supported me more than anyone. Professionally, your creative vision while on shoot was all that I could have wanted for this book, and your support and love in life has shown me what I can achieve. So, thank you from the bottom of my heart.

ENDEMOL SHINE GROUP WOULD LIKE TO THANK...

First and foremost, Franc Roddam for the foreword and the ten *MasterChef* contestants from around the world who contributed to this beautiful collection: Thomas Frake, Lucas Furtado, Alida Gotta, Gabriel Jonsson, Dino Angelo Luciano, Ana Iglesias Panichelli, Smrutisree Singh, Sandy Tang, Simon Toohey and Sowmiya Venkatesan. Also a huge thank you to Adam O'Shepherd for developing recipes that capture the heart of *MasterChef* and his photography.

ABOUT THE AUTHOR

Adam O'Shepherd worked in the restaurant industry for 20 years before stepping out of the kitchen and turning his hand to restaurant consultancy, food styling and recipe development. He developed the award-winning menus for the Bok-Shop in Brighton and Eastbourne, and has recipe tested and styled award-winning cookbooks, including *The Vinegar Cupboard* and *The Botanical Kitchen*.

Having grown up in Australia and worked in kitchens all around the world, including Sydney, Stockholm and London, Adam currently lives in Bristol with his wife and daughter. *MasterChef Green* is his first book.

BLOOMSBURY ABSOLUTE
Bloomsbury Publishing Plc
50 Bedford Square, London, WC1B 3DP, UK
29 Earlsfort Terrace, Dublin 2, Ireland

BLOOMSBURY, BLOOMSBURY ABSOLUTE, the Diana logo and
the Absolute Press logo are trademarks of Bloomsbury Publishing Plc

First published in Great Britain 2021.

A catalogue record for this book is available from the British Library.

Library of Congress Cataloguing-in-Publication data has been applied for.

HB: 9781472978325
ePUB: 9781472978318
ePDF: 9781472978301

2 4 6 8 10 9 7 5 3 1

Printed and bound in China by C&C Offset Printing Co. Ltd

Bloomsbury Publishing Plc makes every effort to ensure that the papers
used in the manufacture of our books are natural, recyclable products made
from wood grown in well-managed forests. Our manufacturing processes
conform to the environmental regulations of the country of origin.

To find out more about our authors and books visit www.bloomsbury.com
and sign up for our newsletters.

Publisher
Jon Croft

Commissioning Editor
Meg Boas

Senior Project Editor
Emily North

Design and Art Direction
Peter Moffat

Photoshoot Art Direction
Marie O'Shepherd

Junior Designer
Anika Schulze

Endemol Shine Group Team
Alice Bernardi, Aimee Joughin,
Claire Morgan and Jane Smith

Photography
Adam and Marie O'Shepherd

Home Economist
Elaine Byfield

Copyeditor
Susan Low

Proofreader
Rachel Malig

Indexer
Zoe Ross